The Practical Handbook of

FURNITURE
REFINISHING
RESTYLING and REPAIR

By John H. Savage

Fawcett Publications, Inc.
1515 Broadway
New York, New York 10036

FRANK BOWERS: *Editor-in-Chief*

SILVIO LEMBO: *Creative Director*

HAROLD E. PRICE: *Associate Director* • HERB JONAS: *Assistant Director*

JOSEPH C. PENELL: *Marketing Director*

RAY GILL: *Editor*

LUCILLE DE SANTIS: *Production Editor*

Editorial Staff: DAN BLUE, ELLENE SAUNDERS, LARRY WERLINE, JULIA BETZ

Art Staff: MIKE GAYNOR, ALEX SANTIAGO, JOHN SELVAGGIO, JOHN CERVASIO, JACK LA CERRA, MIKE MONTE

How-To Art by Henry Clark and Fred Neinast
Photography by Andrew D. Savage

Printed in U.S.A. by
FAWCETT PRINTING CORPORATION
Rockville, Maryland

SECOND PRINTING

CONTENTS

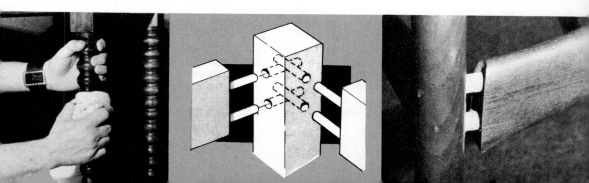

One of the joys of refinishing furniture is being able to bring out the hidden beauty of antiques like this table. Mellow color, rich wood grain were enhanced by new finish.

WHAT YOU'RE GETTING INTO

An overall look at what to expect when you remodel, repair, refinish old furniture.

Refinishing furniture is easy, simple and fun. All you need is a couple of dollars worth of tools and materials, a small space to work in and *patience*.

Of the three, patience is probably the most underrated. Don't neglect it, even if you are known as the "impatient type." Give yourself enough time. Relax. Enjoy your work, and you'll do a better job. Because refinishing is pretty much chemistry at work—and paint removers take time to loosen the paint, glues take time to hold fast, sealers take time to seal and paints, varnishes and lacquers all take time to dry.

The rewards of refinishing are great. You increase the market value of a piece of furniture, to say the least. More impor-

tant, since you probably don't intend to sell it, is the fact that you made the thing into something more beautiful and functional. And probably most important is the sense of accomplishment you get from taking an ugly discard and turning it into something that's valued and even loved.

ANYONE CAN DO IT

What is involved in refinishing? Do you have to be "handy" to do it successfully? Fortunately, refinishing is not difficult. In fact, it can be simple enough for a child to do. Or it can be very complicated and involved, as in the case of a highly polished piano finish, for example.

But the nice thing about refinishing is

that you can do any or all of these things right in your own home. With a very little practice, you will be able to achieve results that are indistinguishable from a professional finish. Because refinishing is so easy and so rewarding when you learn how to do it, it may well be one of the most popular "Underground" hobbies in America.

To refinish a piece of furniture usually involves four things:

1. Removing the old finish
2. Repairing and making structural changes
3. Preparing the wood for a new finish
4. Applying the new finish.

Now, let's take a quick look at what's involved in each of these steps.

STRIPPING

Stripping is what the antique dealers call the process of removing the old paint and varnish. It may be the thing that keeps most people away from refinishing. It used to be a big job.

In the old days, stripping involved days of hand scraping or the use of dangerous caustic chemicals. If you didn't get blisters from the scraper, you'd get them from the chemicals.

That's all changed now. Modern chemical removers are effective, safe and easy to use. The biggest trick to this job is patience. Let the paint remover do the work. That takes 15 to 30 minutes for most types from the time you slop it on with an old brush. When the old paint or varnish becomes soft, you scrape it off with a putty knife into an old coffee can. Then you rub off whatever old paint is left with a coarse cloth or steel wool soaked in water or paint thinner, depending on which type remover it is.

Stripping is best done out of doors or in the basement, since drippings can ruin good floors, tiles and rugs. You can easily strip any article of furniture in a single Saturday afternoon. Which isn't bad considering the stuff may have been on there for a hundred years.

REPAIRING

Don't skip this step. If the piece is in

New chemical paint removers make stripping fairly easy although it can be a bit messy. Key to success is having a place to work and giving remover time to work.

Few materials are needed to strip paint and varnish effectively: a good quality remover, an old brush to apply it with, assorted scrapers, wire brush, steel wool and knife.

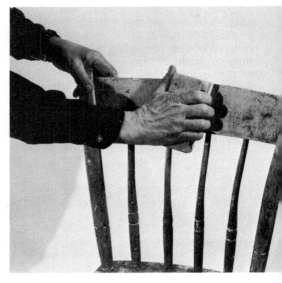

To repair a piece such as this table, it is often necessary to take it apart first. This is usually easier than it looks and makes the finished project as good as new structurally.

Wood preparation is next after stripping. This includes filling cracks and dents and then sanding with progressively finer grits of paper. If not done well, finish will suffer.

such bad shape that you can't fix it yourself, have someone else do it. But don't neglect it, because there's little use in spending the time, money and effort required to create a beautiful finish on a chair with a broken rung, or on a chest of drawers with veneer that has come unglued.

After you've stripped off all the old paint, you'll see better what is wrong with the piece, if anything, and be able to fix it better than with the old paint still on.

What kind of repairs can you expect? A chair rung that has come loose from the leg. Or a back slat that is broken. Or a seat that is split. Bureau drawers may stick. Table legs may be loose. Upholstery may be soiled or torn or sagging. Cane and rush bottoms and backs may be broken. Veneer may be loose. Inlays may be missing. And there may be any number of gouges, dents, cracks, holes, scratches and burns.

You can see that the crafts involved

are many. Naturally, no one person could be expected to learn them all. But you don't have to. You can usually figure out enough about your specific problem to do the repairing yourself, if you want to. Putting in a cane bottom is certainly possible for the average handyman. A little practice can have you putting on veneer. And the woodworking skills needed for most repairs are certainly within the talents of the average refinisher.

RESTYLING

Under the general heading of repairing comes restyling. You'll be getting into the same kind of crafts and use the same kind of skills needed for repairing. Most people have little trouble with the average restyling problems like cutting an old table down to coffee table size or removing the gingerbread from an old dresser.

To do the basic woodworking jobs encountered in repairing and restyling, you

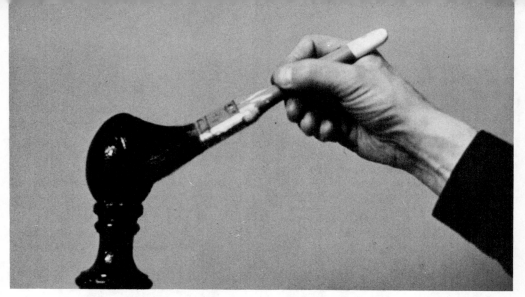

To apply a fine finish, always use a good brush. Work in room that is warm and free of dust and lint. It should also be a low-traffic area where project can remain undisturbed

should have a few tools and a place to work, which is covered farther on.

PREPARING THE WOOD

This is the step which determines what the final finish will look like. If you leave scratches or dents or saw marks, if you do not use the right grades of sandpaper in the right order, if you blotch up the staining or leave tiny fibers or grain standing up, the final finish will show it. And by that time, there's nothing to be done except strip it down again and start over.

After you've made all necessary repairs, filled all cracks and dents and removed every last trace of the old finish, start sanding. Begin with coarse paper, use intermediate grades and end with a fine grade. Then stain, if you like, and resand. On certain open-grained woods, you can apply a cream-like filler, which should then be resanded. Finally, a sealer such as shellac or special sealer compounds is applied and sanded once again. Then you're ready for the final finish.

The wood preparation stage can be done almost anywhere but for best results, it should be someplace reasonably warm, lint free and undisturbed during the process.

APPLYING THE FINAL FINISH

There are hundreds of finishes that you can apply. Some are commercial preparations. Others you make up yourself. Some can be brushed on and used after a couple of hours. Others must be put on in layers with much hand rubbing in between. Some finishes are clear and reveal the beauty of the wood. Others are opaque and conceal its defects. Some finishes are durable. Others fragile. There is a place for each. And perhaps the most difficult job you'll have is deciding which finish you should use.

For the final finishing, the work area is important. Warm, dust-and-lint-free surroundings are essential to promote optimum drying times and keep the wet surface away from the danger of being marred by things landing on it.

As for the tools and materials, they consist of a good brush, some soft, clean cloths, perhaps some very fine grades of sandpaper and steel wool, rubbing oil if called for and of course the finishing material itself, along with appropriate thinners.

These are the basic steps. Most people enjoy doing them. And the results are sure to delight and please you.

A permanent place to work is important if you intend to do more than occasional repair or refinishing projects. This crude but effective workshop is set up in corner of garage.

WORKBENCH AND TOOLS

A place to work and the means to get the job done are the subjects discussed here

This section will cover a lot of tools and equipment. But that's not because you need them all. Or even a large number of them. You definitely do not. The reason for covering so many is to ac-quaint you with what's available. You just might see the ideal tool for a tricky job. Then you can borrow or buy it. You're certain to see some basic tools you already have, or intend to get. So don't

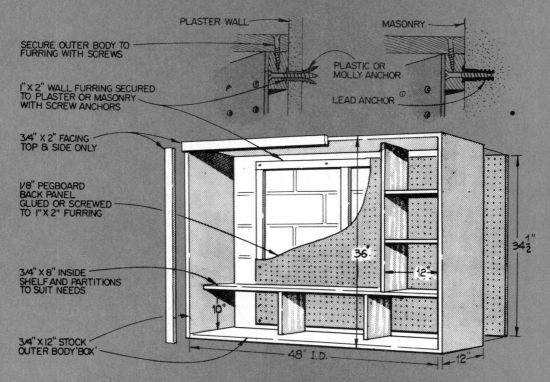

SECURE OUTER BODY TO
FURRING WITH SCREWS

PLASTER WALL

MASONRY

PLASTIC OR
MOLLY ANCHOR

LEAD ANCHOR

1" X 2" WALL FURRING SECURED
TO PLASTER OR MASONRY
WITH SCREW ANCHORS

3/4" X 2" FACING
TOP & SIDE ONLY

1/8" PEGBOARD
BACK PANEL
GLUED OR SCREWED
TO 1" X 2" FURRING

3/4" X 8" INSIDE
SHELF AND PARTITIONS
TO SUIT NEEDS

3/4" X 12" STOCK
OUTER BODY 'BOX'

36"

12"

$34\frac{1}{2}$"

10"

48" I.D.

12"

Four-foot workbench and overhead cabinets are easy to build and do not take up much space, yet they serve almost all the work space needs for repair and refinishing projects.

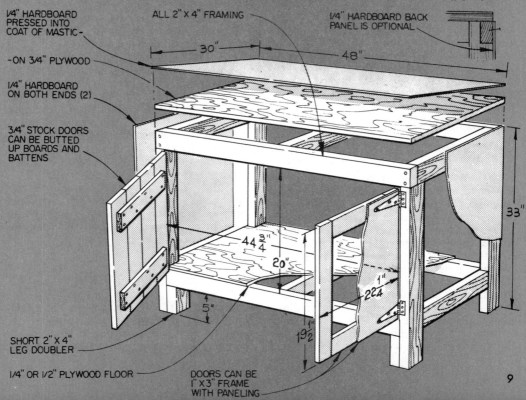

1/4" HARDBOARD
PRESSED INTO
COAT OF MASTIC

ALL 2" X 4" FRAMING

1/4" HARDBOARD BACK
PANEL IS OPTIONAL

-ON 3/4" PLYWOOD

30"

48"

1/4" HARDBOARD
ON BOTH ENDS (2)

3/4" STOCK DOORS
CAN BE BUTTED
UP BOARDS AND
BATTENS

$44\frac{3}{4}$"

20"

$1\frac{1}{2}$
$22\frac{1}{4}$

33"

5"

$19\frac{1}{2}$

SHORT 2" X 4"
LEG DOUBLER

1/4" OR 1/2" PLYWOOD FLOOR

DOORS CAN BE
1" X 3" FRAME
WITH PANELING

9

Furniture platform in use. Surface should be flat and level so furniture being glued will not set up crooked. Drop cloth is used over carpeting when finishes are applied.

Dovetail saw is rarely found in home tool kit but it is invaluable for the fine cutting required by furniture repair work. Other special inexpensive tools are also helpful.

think you have to get fancy with a big shop and lots of tools. You don't. Perfectly sound repairs have been made with nothing more than Elmer's Glue and three feet of clothesline rope.

When acquiring tools, whether one-at-a-time or together in a kit, always try to get good ones. It's difficult and sometimes impossible to do good work with cheap, inadequate tools.

THE WORK AREA

You don't have to have a shop, but you do have to have a place to work. Maybe it's the kitchen counter with your tools kept in the back of a drawer. Or maybe it's a 30-foot basement. It should have these things: warmth because most finishes and glues dry faster and better the warmer it is; clean air because dust and lint will land on wet finishes and ruin them; light because you can't do fine work and you can't judge colors in light that is inadequate or light that throws strong shadows; and electricity both for light and for any power tools you have.

THE WORKBENCH

It all depends on the space you have, of course. Its height should be from 33″ to 36″ depending on your height. The top should be about 24″ from back to front, and the length can be just about anything you like.

Whatever its size, the work surface must be quite solid, at least an inch thick and with solid underpinnings. It must have heavy enough framing to support a woodworkers vise solidly.

Below the bench should be an enclosed storage area for tools and materials.

Build shelves with doors above the workbench for easy access to your tools and supplies. A tip: keep each tool in its own place to save hunting for it at the time you need it most.

A FINISHING PLATFORM

If you work on furniture much, either building it new or refinishing it, a low covered platform is helpful. It lets you get at big pieces more easily than you could

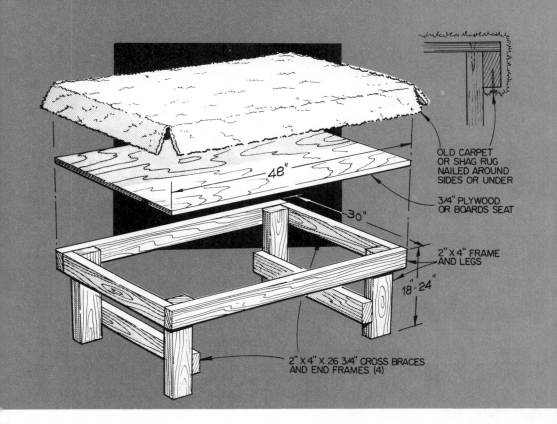

OLD CARPET
OR SHAG RUG
NAILED AROUND
SIDES OR UNDER

3/4" PLYWOOD
OR BOARDS SEAT

48"

30"

2" X 4" FRAME
AND LEGS

18 - 24"

2" X 4" X 26 3/4" CROSS BRACES
AND END FRAMES (4)

Easily-constructed finishing platform raises furniture project to handy height for working. Old carpeting protects furniture being repaired but isn't needed for just refinishing jobs.

on the floor or on your workbench. The old carpeting cover prevents marring the wood or finish on the piece you're working on.

A PAINT LOCKER

It's a good idea to keep your paint and supplies in one place . . . a place where it won't freeze. A shelf, cabinet, cupboard or almost anything will do. One area should be reserved for non-liquid supplies like sandpaper, steel wool, scrapers, sanders, brushes and the like. Another area should be reserved for liquids you use frequently such as thinners, linseed oil, sealers and stains.

When it comes to paints, varnishes, lacquers, shellac and other materials for finishing, it isn't good to keep them very long. White masking tape makes a fine label for dating each bottle and can.

Don't be afraid to throw away half empty cans of hardened, separated finishing materials.

WOODWORKING TOOLS

A box of tools which is fine for average household chores, or for heavy carpentry work, may not be very helpful in repairing and restyling furniture. Generally speaking, the tools you will need are those of the cabinetmaker. This means that they are smaller, make finer, more precise cuts and produce smoother surfaces.

Remember, if you do much furniture repairing, you'll end up using all kinds of tools, some for crafts you probably never dreamed of doing. The descriptions that follow are merely to help you select those that might be most helpful.

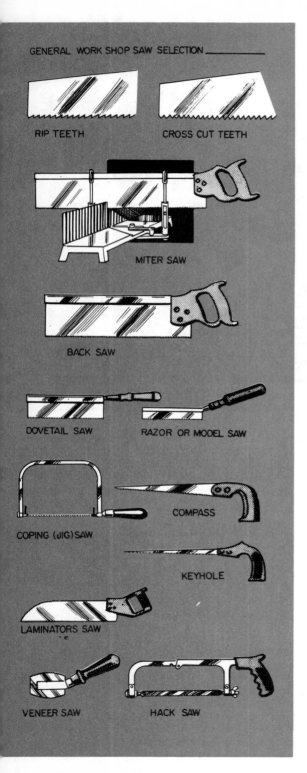

GENERAL WORK SHOP SAW SELECTION

RIP TEETH CROSS CUT TEETH

MITER SAW

BACK SAW

DOVETAIL SAW RAZOR OR MODEL SAW

COPING (JIG) SAW COMPASS

KEYHOLE

LAMINATORS SAW

VENEER SAW HACK SAW

SAWS

A big 24″ carpenter's handsaw with 8 teeth to the inch is not often helpful in repairing furniture. For precise cuts, much smaller saws are used.

Back saws—in order of fineness of cut they are **razor saw, veneer saw, dovetail saw,** and **miter box saw.** The smallest is just an inch long by ¾″ wide. The largest can be as long as 30″. Range of points per inch is 12 to more than 20. Back saws are so called because of a reinforcing rib along the back. They make precise straight cuts which can be very smooth.

Coping saw—it's the "D" shaped frame with the ⅛″ blade held in tension. Cuts sharp turns nicely. Not very smooth.

Keyhole saw—available in various sizes. Pointed blade handy for cutting irregular shapes and tricky holes.

Veneer saw—some versions are double bladed and razor thin. Used to cut against a steel straightedge. Sharp, precise cuts.

Hack saw—for cutting metal. Blades are available in a variety of teeth per inch. Used frequently in repair work for things like cutting off corroded nuts and bolts.

CUTTING TOOLS

In repair work, you are frequently faced with carving or cutting strange shapes so many different tools can be used.

Pocket knife—the so-called "Stockman's" knife is handiest with three blades of different shapes.

X-Acto knife—the model makers favorite has a big brother that's handy in repair work. Basically an interchangeable razor-like blade with a good handle.

CARVING TOOLS

Used anywhere a small chisel is needed. Fine quality steel is sharper and stays sharper than carpenter's chisels. Usually come six to a set with several flat blades and several that scoop.

Wood chisels—for heavier work than carving tools, but still needed often for furniture repair work. A set usually comes in ⅛″ graduations from ¼″ width up to 2″. In selecting a chisel, it's width should be about half that of the cut to be made.

SMOOTHING TOOLS

These are the planes, shaves and scrapers which are indispensible to the furniture repairer and restyler.

Block plane—a baby plane designed for cutting across end grain. Also handy for small work such as reducing thickness of patches.

Smoothing plane—this is the carpenter's basic plane and in the smaller sizes it's handy for repairing. Large sizes can be used to reduce thickness of large boards, if and when that becomes necessary.

Jack plane—a bigger, slightly different configuration of the smoothing plane. Longer length skips over low spots, cuts off high spots, making for a more even cut.

Spoke shave—like a block plane with ears, and you draw it toward you. Very handy for delicate work.

Cabinet scraper—looks like a spoke shave, but for even more delicate work. It's the finest cut of all, used to remove marks left by plane.

Hand scraper—hard steel sheets, either straight edged or with concave and convex curves. Edge is squared and burnished to produce a hook or burred edge which is pulled over the wood surface to produce a very smooth texture. Used for veneers where a plane might cut too deep.

Glass scraper—a piece of broken glass, of the proper shape, makes a fine hand scraper and is used as above. Wear work gloves and discard the glass once it becomes dull.

TOOLS FOR MAKING HOLES

Brace and bit—ancient system for making holes, still works well. Recommended for larger sized holes since it can be controlled well.

Hand drill—the manual version of the electric drill, with all of its faults and none of its virtues.

HAMMERS

There seems to be a special hammer designed for every craft known to man. They aren't used much in repair work, but when they're needed you gotta have one.

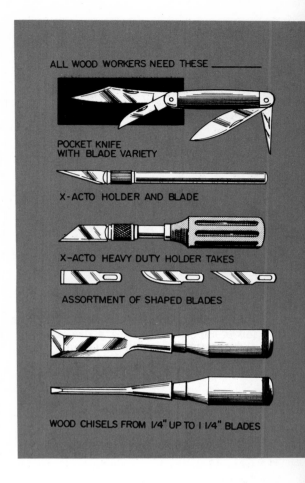

ALL WOOD WORKERS NEED THESE ⎯⎯⎯⎯⎯

POCKET KNIFE WITH BLADE VARIETY

X-ACTO HOLDER AND BLADE

X-ACTO HEAVY DUTY HOLDER TAKES

ASSORTMENT OF SHAPED BLADES

WOOD CHISELS FROM 1/4" UP TO 1 1/4" BLADES

A fine quality block plane is not expensive, yet it's invaluable for repair work. Always keep the blade razor sharp because a dull blade can cause more damage than help.

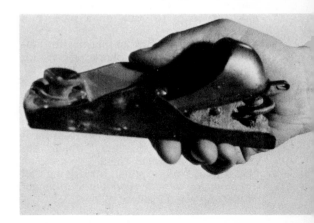

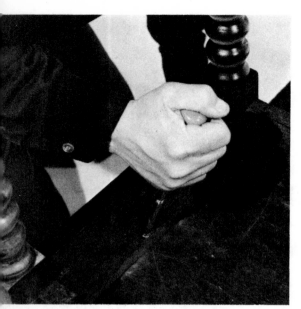

Having the right screwdriver size for the job is important. Too big a size won't fit and too small size might chew up screw head. Screws were re-used many times.

Get good ones and lots of them. To turn in a screw, or turn it out, select a screw driver with a tip that exactly matches the slot in the screw, both in width and length. Otherwise, you may chew up the screw slot. The longer the blade of the screw driver, the easier it will be to turn. The sides of the tip should be as nearly parallel as possible. Tapering sides will cause the tip to rise out of the slot.

Yankee Rachet Screwdriver—Highly recommended is the rachet-type screwdriver like the famous "Yankee". By simply pushing, you can turn screws either in or out. The downward energy is converted to torque by the rachet and by flipping a switch, you can change the direction from clockwise to counterclockwise. Or, you can make it rigid. It also doubles as a small drill. There are a wide assortment of screwdriver and drill bits available for the "Yankee", including Phillips head screwdrivers. It's one tool that serves as a whole collection.

OTHER TOOLS

Carpenter's hammer—there is the claw hammer for pulling nails and the rip hammer for tearing things up. Weights range from 13 oz. to 20 oz. or more. Great for building houses, can be used in your shop.

Ball-peen hammer—one spherical head, one flat. Designed for machinists, useful for a host of things including riveting.

Small sledge—great when you need the mass of metal to back up a piece and pound against.

Mallet—heavy woods or plastic, for impact without marring work. Good for driving in dowels.

Soft-faced hammer—for metal work where it is important not to dent or mar work. Face may be leather or plastic.

Tack hammer—handy little hammer with magnetic end for holding tacks. Similar is the upholsterer's hammer, which has faces at a more acute angle.

Nail set—a kind of punch for driving nail in below the wood surface without danger of marring wood itself.

Pliers—not officially a woodworking tool but they come in handy. As astonishing variety, too, from the 10-cent store combination plier to delicate curved needle point plier. Consider the powerful gripping plier for tremendous holding power, or the groove-joint type pliers like those made by Channel lock.

Wrenches—basic types are adjustable, open end, box and socket. When faced with jobs like turning off the nut from a rusty old bolt holding on a table leg, having the right wrench is essential. But basically they belong in the mechanic's tool box. Occasionally, a socket wrench proves helpful in reaching into tight places.

Snips, nippers and cutters—all these tools come in handy but are not essential. Nippers and cutters for wire and nail heads, snips for sheet metal.

Rasps and files—metal files are essential for sharpening saws and sometimes plane irons and chisels. Coarser cuts can be used for shaping wood, as well. Rasps are

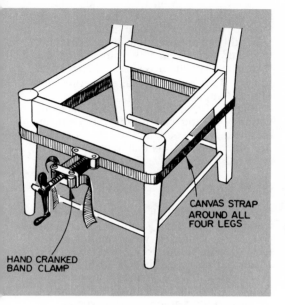

HAND CRANKED
BAND CLAMP

CANVAS STRAP
AROUND ALL
FOUR LEGS

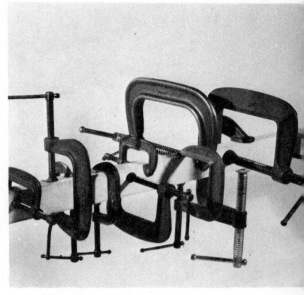

A hand clamp is ideal for hard-to-hold pieces such as this chair frame, round table tops or other irregular shapes. Always check for squareness after clamp is tight.

C-clamps in sizes from 2″ to 8″ or 12″ should be in every repair tool box because nearly every joint should be glued under pressure. Spring clips are for light pressure.

very coarse and for wood and plastic only. Because a rasp removes so much wood so brutally, they aren't recommended for cabinet work. Curved riffler files are great for finishing irregular spots.

Clamps—this is a big subject in repair work. There are, fortunately, hundreds of types and sooner or later, they are all required for some job. They divide up basically into C-clamps, bar clamps, hand screws, press screws, band clamps, spring clamps, tourniquets and wedges. C-clamps are most common and range in size from 1″ to 6″, with larger sizes sometimes available. When you get into larger work, however, the bar clamp and pipe clamp are used. The bar clamp is a standard item in cabinetmakers' shops and the pipe clamp is an ingenious and inexpensive version of it. You buy the clamp fixture for about $5 and fit it to any old length of ¾″ pipe.

A band clamp is a length of pre-stretched 2″ canvas with a screw tighten-

ing mechanism. Usually, they are about 15′ long. For large, irregular shapes, chair legs, etc. Unless great pressure is required, a tourniquet of clothesline rope will often do the job as well.

Spring clamps are like large metal clothespins and can be used quickly where great pressure is not essential. Press screws are simply screws, handles and bushing which can be installed in a home made frame of any size. Designed for veneering, but handy for lots of cabinet work.

A hand screw is an important tool in cabinet work, too, because it can clamp work which has sides that are not parallel. By turning the front screw more or less than the back screw, a wide variety of angles are produced. Size range is from 6″ to 14″.

Wedges are also important is clamping work and can be made at home. For example, a big "U" shape cut from plywood and a couple of wedges make a fine "C" clamp. A sheet of ½″ plywood with

15

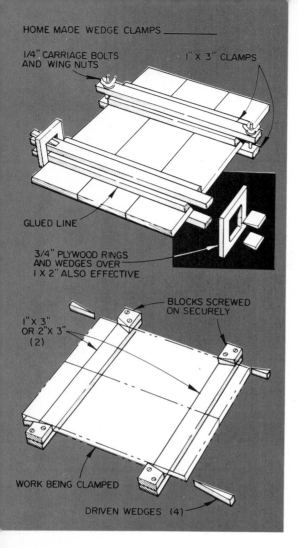

1/4" CARRIAGE BOLTS AND WING NUTS

1" X 3" CLAMPS

GLUED LINE

3/4" PLYWOOD RINGS AND WEDGES OVER 1 X 2" ALSO EFFECTIVE

BLOCKS SCREWED ON SECURELY

1" X 3" OR 2" X 3" (2)

WORK BEING CLAMPED

DRIVEN WEDGES (4)

Table leaf being held by home-made wedge clamps, made as required in a few minutes from scrap lumber. For many gluing jobs, home-made clamps work as well as any.

blocks screwed or clamped down makes a neat temporary bar clamp. You'll be able to figure out many ways to solve specific clamping problems with wedges if you don't have the right commercial clamping device on hand.

Shapes are important, too. These are irregular blocks used between a clamp and irregular work so the clamp can get a grip on the surface. Usually, shapes must be cut specifically for the work in prog-

ress, but a few V-groove blocks, round-groove blocks and blocks that can be cut to shape should be kept on hand.

Sand bags are used like shapes. Make a few sand bags from light canvas and use them against an irregular shape, with square block on top to take the pressure of the clamp.

Picture frame clamps come in many varieties or you can make your own, either using plywood and wedges or with 36" threaded rods available at most hardware stores.

A VISE

Since it is difficult to work on either wood or metal that is not securely held, you really should have a small vise for each. A wide-faced woodworkers vise and a machinist's type bench vise, respectively. Although the former can cost more than $50 and the latter more than $200, a small workshop grade of each type can be purchased for under $10 and will be good enough for almost all repair work you're likely to get into. If you have to make a choice, take the woodworker vise.

TOOLS FOR GLUING

A cheap, invaluable tool is the glue injector. You can buy a metal one that looks like a syringe for $2. Or get a big plastic medical syringe. Used to squirt glue into veneer bubbles and loose corners.

For your information, there are electric glue pots on the market which keep up to a quart of hot glue on hand. Fine for veneering and furniture production, but not needed by the repair worker.

A glue gun is another story, however. It works on 110-volt current. You load a pellet or stick of hard glue into the rear of the gun and push and out of the nozzel comes hot glue. Advantage of hot glue is its accelerated bonding time. Some manufacturers claim that it will make a tight bond in 60 seconds without clamping. At any rate, it does speed up small gluing jobs.

MEASURING TOOLS

In addition to the folding rules, steel rules and various squares, woodworkers can make good use of several other types of measuring tool: inside-outside calipers, dividers, marking gage, contour gage. Calipers are for accurate measurement of cylindrical pieces and holes, mortises and tenons, etc. Dividers can be used to transfer measurements and for copying contours. A marking gage is used to scripe a line at a fixed measurement. A contour gage is a rather new device made of many fine wires which can be pushed to conform to almost any shape with great accuracy.

POWER TOOLS

There is an amazing variety of power tools available to the home craftsman, both stationary tools and portable ones. While they are all fun and frequently handy, there are only a couple which are *really needed* by the occasional woodworker. The ¼-inch electric drill, the electric grinder and perhaps the saber saw. Small electric drills have become very inexpensive—even less than the price of a top-quality hand drill—and they do a wide variety of jobs well. Drilling is obviously the main job, but they can be used with grinding wheels, polishers, sanders, routers and many other accessories.

An electric grinder is probably less necessary but is recommended because when you have it you'll keep all your cutting tools sharper and therefore do better work in every phase of a job. Note that a grinder should not be used for the final sharpening, but only to set the angle of a blade and get it square and true. The final edge is put on with an oil stone.

A saber saw is often recommended for the home woodworker because it can do a lot of jobs you'd have trouble doing with a coping saw. And, of course, it saves you work.

An electric sander is also valuable to the refinisher, but perhaps not as handy for fine work as you'd expect. Belt sanders are too crude and powerful for fine cabinet work. They cut too fast. Orbital sanders do produce a nice oscillating motion but changing the sandpaper every few minutes can be as much work as just sanding by hand. If you do large areas

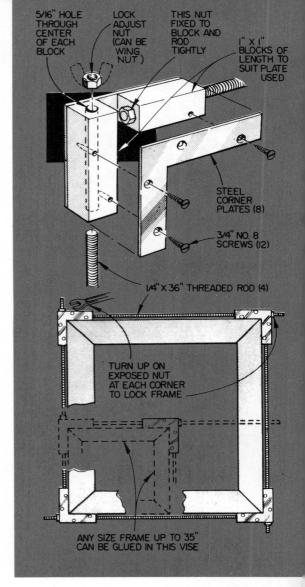

Picture frame clamp can be made from threaded rods, steel angles and wood blocks at little cost. When fastening frame with nails, keep pieces square and flat.

frequently, they are definitely in order, though.

Remember that there is no such thing as a power tool you have to have. Especially in furniture repair, anything can be

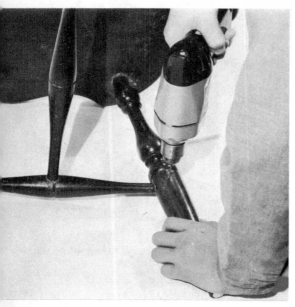

Most craftsmen rate the electric drill as the #1 power tool. Here, it is used to drill for the pin to hold chair rung. The many other uses include sanding, polishing, grinding.

done with hand tools. But power tools can definitely make the job go faster and be more fun.

TOOLS FOR REFINISHING

Compared to woodworking, there is very little hardware required for finishing. And most of them wear out rapidly compared to woodworking tools. Nevertheless, you should use top quality products, especially brushes.

Brushes—for fine finishes, stick to bristle brushes of good quality. Even the best bristle brushes come in several grades, usually a utility grade for basic varnish, paint, enamel, lacquer and other finishes; and an especially fine grade with softer bristle ox-hair for flowing on finishes when fineness is required.

A good utility grade bristle brush 3″ wide can cost over $5 and an extra fine bristle brush may cost as much as $9. They are worth it.

For applying paint and varnish remov-ers for stripping, any old brush will do. Or one of the ten-cent store cheapies.

After using a brush, clean it thoroughly. Work out as much of the paint, varnish or whatever you were using it with on an old board. Work again after soaking in the solvent for the finishing material. In most cases, the brush can be washed in soap and water after as much finish as possible is removed.

An easier way to clean a brush is with a commercial preparation like Klean-Strip Brush Cleaner. The chemicals emul-sify the paint, varnish, lacquer, shellac or whatever, so it will wash out with water. It's a good idea to comb out the bristles as you wash the brush.

When do you discard a brush? When it doesn't do a good job. If the bristles fall out, or become frayed and wild, or if the bristle layers become separated so it won't hold the finishing material, it should be discarded or relegated to paint remover work.

Scrapers—these range from elaborate handles with interchangeable blades, to pieces of broken glass. There are two types: one for scraping off paint and var-nish after the removers have been ap-plied; and the other for scraping down and smoothing bare wood. A paint scraper should not be used on untreated paint or other finish. It's a lot of work and you can nick and gouge the wood surface badly. Always use some sort of remover to soften the finish.

Smoothing scrapers are used on raw wood. A cabinet scraper is really a little plane, like a spoke shave, and will make a very fine cut. Hand scrapers are pieces of tempered steel (often made from old saw blades) cut to shapes and burnished with a slight hook to the edge. They are pulled with the grain at a slight angle from verti-cal and produce very fine shavings. There are hand scrapers shaped for many types of inside and outside curves. They are "sharpened" by putting the hooked edge on again with a hard steel rod called a burnisher.

The woodened handled scrapers are not used for cabinet work but are handy for paint removal in conjunction with paint removers. They must be kept sharp with a fine mill file, maintaining the clean, slightly angled edge.

It is virtually impossible to put on a fine finish with a bad brush. The time and effort you put into your project always justifies the expense of the best brush you can get.

Putty knife—for scraping off paint and varnish that has been softened by removers. Less dangerous to the wood beneath than the big scrapers. Also used for applying patching materials to dents, cracks and holes.

Spatula—used for applying patching material, including stick shellac to holes and dents.

ALCOHOL LAMP

Used for heating spatula or putty knife when applying stick shellac. Why not a gas stove? It makes soot which is deposited on the blade. Alcohol lamps do not.

SANDERS

A block of wood makes a good hand sander. A block of wood with a felt or rubber pad between it and the paper is even better. Paint stores sell a number of commercial hand sanders, including those with rolls of sandpaper which can be fed out as it wears. Generally speaking, the simpler the better. It should be straight and square and have some kind of thin cushioning to even out small depressions and irregularities, no matter how microscopic.

Electric belt sanders accomplish a lot in the way of rough cutting, but should only be used on solid raw wood in the coarses stages of reduction. Never use an electric sander on veneer.

Electric disc sanders, as used on electric drills, are not recommended for cabinet work. They cut too fast and produce scratches in all directions. All sanding must be done with the grain.

Orbital sanders, as mentioned earlier, produce a nice rotating sanding action and when used with the best grade of sandpaper can be a great labor-saver. For small jobs, changing the papers may be more work than just sanding by hand.

An assortment of scrapers and putty knives are handy for removing paint and varnish after the chemical strippers are applied. File corners so they will not dig into the wood.

Three basic electric sanders are: rotating (front), reciprocal (left) and belt (right). Rotating sander leaves cross-grain marks and even the best is a bit hard to control.

When properly repaired and refinished, old furniture can be as functional and beautiful as when it was made, or even better. And the money you save doing it yourself is important too.

CHAIR AND TABLE REPAIRS

You can always make it good as new, sometimes better

There is no piece of furniture in such bad shape that you can't make it as good as, or better than new. The catch is: would it be worth it. Sometimes you have to jack up the tabletop and run a new frame under it. But then, some tabletops are so beautiful, it's worth doing. On the other hand, there are priceless antiques which would be improved *structurally* by a thorough repair job but that would ruin its value as an antique.

In this section, most of the problems involve woodworking because that's what most furniture is made of. There are a couple of allied topics, however, like basic upholstering and basic chair caning. The first topic you should know about is adhesives.

GLUING

It may be the oldest form of fastening, with the possible exception of rawhide or vines. And it's also the newest. Developments in chemistry have made it possible to glue together houses, airplanes, boats and, of course, furniture.

There are many types and a lot of glues are made from secret formulas, so it's sometimes hard to categorize them. The basic types often required by the home woodworker are: Hide (or animal) glue; white (polyvinyl) glue; casein glue; plastic resin glue; urea-resin glue, resorcinol and epoxy. Two other types found in the average household are cellulose (or "airplane") glue and mucilage. The Glue

TYPES AND USES OF ADHESIVES

TYPE	FORM	STRENGTH	USES	WATER RESISTANCE	HEAT RESISTANCE	TEMPERATURE (MINIMUM)	TIME IN CLAMPS TO CURE	GLUELINE APPEARANCE
Hide (or animal) Glue	Liquid (often used hot)	Good	Furniture, musical instruments	Poor	Poor	70°	3 hrs. — 24 hrs.	Light tan or colorless
White Glue (polyvinyl)	Liquid	Fair	Light cabinet work, where little strain is encountered. Also models, labels, etc.	Poor	Poor	50°	30 mins. — 24 hrs.	Clear
Casein Glue	Powder (mix with water)	Good	Outdoor furniture, oily woods like teak. Heavy duty repairs. Fills voids, good for loose joints. Not for veneers.	Good to Fair	Good	70°	4 hrs. — 24 hrs.	Light—tends to stain certain woods
Plastic Resin Glue	Powder (mix with water)	Very Good	Furniture, indoor work, fabric, leather, porous materials. For tight joints only. Will not fill voids well. Not for oily woods.	Very Good	Good	70°	12 hrs. — 24 hrs.	Light to colorless
Urea-Resin Glue	Powder	Good	Furniture, veneers. Not for outdoor veneering work.	Very good to excellent	Low	70°F.	2 hrs. — 7 hrs.	Colorless to light tan
Resorcinol	Liquid 2 parts must be mixed	Very Good	Outdoor work, boat work, furniture—very durable, heavy duty adhesive laminating—plastics, crockery.	Excellent	Excellent	70°	10 hrs.	Dark Reddish
Epoxy	2 part liquid must be mixed	Excellent	Anything-to-anything. Even metal-to-metal. Available in putty like form for filling voids. China, glass.	Excellent (best)	Good	70°	3 hrs. — 24 hrs.	Medium Dark

Not all table legs are held by glue, dowels or mortised joints. The legs of this typical dining table come right off by removing the nut from hanger bolt in leg. Tap out and pull.

Loose veneer ends are glued and clamped under pressure. Heat speeds glue drying. Use wax paper to prevent clamp boards from sticking. Sand away paper and excess glue.

Chart details the properties of the first seven. The other two may come in handy in a specific instance, but in general are not recommended.

The glues covered in the chart are all used with clamps and clamping times are

given for room temperature of 70°. But it is *important* to understand that all these glues set faster, cure faster and hold better at higher temperatures. There are limits, of course, and some will start to break down again at 150° F. A heat lamp on the glued joint will both speed up and improve your glue joining.

REPAIRING VENEERS

Your veneer problems will probably fall into one of two categories: veneer that has come unglued, and veneer that has broken off.

Unglued veneer can almost always be reglued with little difficulty. The important thing to remember is to clean out the old glue and any dirt, oil, food particles and other stuff that may have worked its way in. If you don't, the new glue won't stick either.

Glue can be injected under the veneer in a number of ways. You can always work it under with a small brush but you must make certain it does not leave bristles behind. Even a whittled down stick is good enough for poking glue under some loose veneers. A better way is to inject it with a small oil can. But if there has been oil in the can first, make sure to get it *perfectly* clean before putting glue in it. You can buy plastic syringes at some drug stores that are suitable for injecting glue, and there are also special glue injectors that are inexpensive.

A frequent veneer fault is a bubble or blister. The glue comes loose, the wood fibers swell and the veneer bubbles up. Sometimes it splits. If so, it may be dirty underneath, and it must be cleaned out completely. In cases where the bubble has not split, make a small incision with a razor or knife to work the glue under the veneer. Press down after the glue has been injected so the excess will flow out. Place wax paper or craft paper over the glued spot, block it and clamp. If the loose veneer is in the center of a tabletop or other spot which cannot be reached by clamping, use heavy weights or, better, place 2x4s across the top and bottom and clamp them with C-clamps, if the gap is small enough, or pipe or bar clamps.

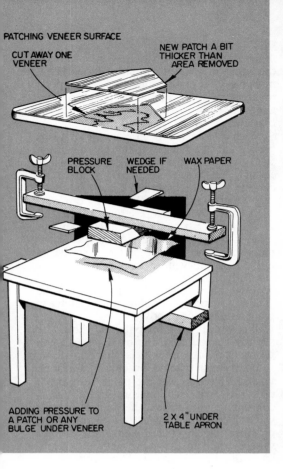

PATCHING VENEER SURFACE

CUT AWAY ONE VENEER

NEW PATCH A BIT THICKER THAN AREA REMOVED

PRESSURE BLOCK

WEDGE IF NEEDED

WAX PAPER

ADDING PRESSURE TO A PATCH OR ANY BULGE UNDER VENEER

2 X 4" UNDER TABLE APRON

Glue dries faster under heat lamp, here applied to table leg-to-apron joint. Photo lamp works almost as well. Glued joints should be held under pressure till dry.

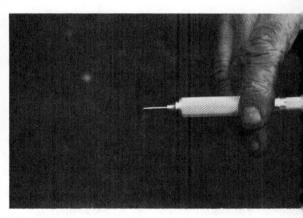

Glue injector is actually a syringe with a hollow needle. Squeeze the plunger and glue comes out. Other glue injectors made of plastic are obtainable at supply stores.

Glue injector in use to fasten down bubbled up veneering. Area under veneer must be clean and grease-free or glue will not hold to the base wood. Weight down or clamp.

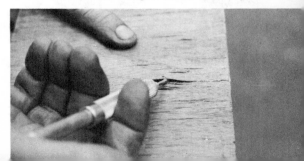

When the glue has thoroughly set, remove pressure device and sand away the paper backing.

BROKEN VENEER

Veneer on edges, corners and curves tend to break off. And the missing piece is long gone. Don't despair. Find a piece and make a patch. Perhaps finding a piece is as simple as prying it loose from another part of the furniture, where it won't show. But veneer is there only for show, so that is not likely. Another source of old veneer is junk shops, where a cheap, broken article may have the kind you want. Otherwise, you'll have to get the wood to match and cut your own. It is not difficult when the broken place is not large. If it is, buy a sheet of veneer to match.

Matching is important if you want to

To make a veneer patch select wood with grain and color that match old wood. Cut the patch large enough to cover the bad spot. It is important to first cut the patch.

Lay veneer patch over the blemished part of the veneer and scribe a line around. This must be done very carefully or the patch will not fit. Cut with razor and steel rule.

maintain the looks. Not only should it be the same wood, but the same type. Thus, mahogany is not sufficient. Philippean mahogany won't match African mahogany. Also, try to match the grain as closely as possible.

With a veneer knife, razor saw or razor blade, cut the veneer patch first. Use a steel straight edge. It should be large enough to cover the broken area, of course. The patch should be cut to an irregular shape so it will be less obvious. That does not mean a free form shape, but a trapezoid, triangle, parallelogram or other shape with straight lines. Place the patch over the broken spot and scribe its outline on the veneer with a knife. Very carefully, cut exactly along those lines and remove the veneer inside. Clean the ground wood and glue the patch in place as described above.

The veneer used for patching should be slightly thicker than the original so it can be sanded flush after it is glued in place.

For veneer patches on curven surfaces, you will have to wet the patch to make it take the shape without breaking. With a contour gauge, trace the curve onto a wood block and saw it out to make the pressure block. Then clamp the wetted veneer patch to the curve without glue to let it dry in that shape. Then glue as described above.

CHAIRS

A well designed chair is a remarkable thing. Some are still in use today after 150 or 200 years. And others will crumble under the weight of a 12-year-old boy.

The reason for this difference in durability is two-fold: design and material. In repair work, there is little you can do about either but it is mentioned so you won't blame yourself for a chair that won't stay fixed. There are chairs like that.

And no wonder. When you lean back in a dining chair, for example, you are creating leverages that are perfect for breaking it. Either by twisting the turned and mortised joints out of their holes, or actually breaking the legs, back and rungs.

Trial fit of patch into base veneering. If cutting and scribing was done carefully and accurately, there should be no need to trim. Next step is to glue patch and base wood.

Press veneer patch in place and wipe away any excess glue that oozes out. Veneer patches are always cut irregularly so they will be unobtrusive when sanded and finished.

Side-to-side sway is a frequent fault of chairs with solid wood (or plank) seats. It is a natural ailment of old age. See drawing.

Trauma happens to chairs just as to humans, usually in the form of a human concentrating his weight onto a single rung or jumping onto a plank seat which splits. See drawing.

RUNG AND SPINDLE REPAIR

This type repair involved a turned end joined in a hole. Repairs involve looseness, usually, but sometimes with broken ends.

Chair leg-to-seat—sway causes the legs to "work" in the holes. The holes enlarge and must be tightened. A quick and easy way to make the holes tighter is with epoxy putty. It holds well and is harder than the surrounding wood. Another solution is to make a hardwood patch which is mortised into the seat bottom where the old hole was. Then a new hole is drilled for the leg. When the amount of looseness is not so great, use casein glue and pin the joint with a small dowel or nail inserted in holed drilled at a 45° angle.

Leg to rung—a sure cure for looseness is cross-doweling. Clean out hole and turned end. Insert with casein glue (or resin glue if the joint is fairly tight) and clamp. Then drill an 1/8" hole through the leg and turned end of the rung. Insert dowel, well glued. Nails have also been used the same way, with the ends filed flush.

Wedged ends—just split the end of the rung or leg carefully. Cut a thin wedge as

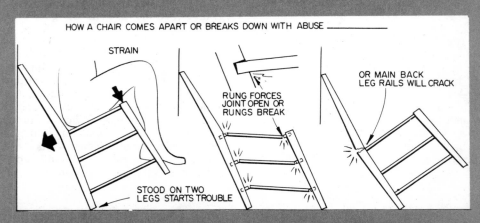

HOW A CHAIR COMES APART OR BREAKS DOWN WITH ABUSE

STRAIN

RUNG FORCES JOINT OPEN OR RUNGS BREAK

OR MAIN BACK LEG RAILS WILL CRACK

STOOD ON TWO LEGS STARTS TROUBLE

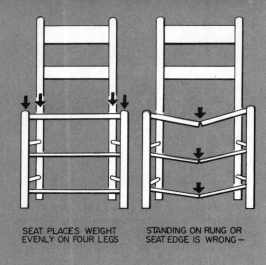

SEAT PLACES WEIGHT
EVENLY ON FOUR LEGS

STANDING ON RUNG OR
SEAT EDGE IS WRONG—

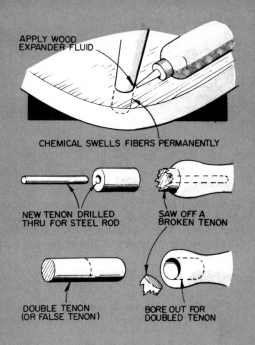

APPLY WOOD
EXPANDER FLUID

CHEMICAL SWELLS FIBERS PERMANENTLY

NEW TENON DRILLED
THRU FOR STEEL ROD

SAW OFF A
BROKEN TENON

DOUBLE TENON
(OR FALSE TENON)

BORE OUT FOR
DOUBLED TENON

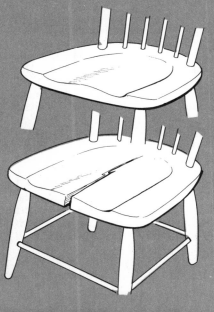

Split in plank seat chair follows grain and makes it unusable. Glue and clamp the seat after making certain that all dirt, grease and loose wood fibers are removed from split.

MORTISE AND TENON JOINTS

This is the square peg in the square hole. Most antique furniture used mortise and tenon joints (in addition to spindle-type joints) instead of a couple of dowels in a butt joint. Mortise and tenon joints hold extremely well, especially if fitted to close tolerances. In the old days, the glues would not make up for the cabinetmakers mistakes, so he had to do good work. Today, lapses can be filled with the new glues.

How can you tell a mortise and tenon joint from a doweled butt joint? You can't always, but if there is a small dowel through one of the pieces where a tenon would be, you can be pretty sure that there is a mortise there. When it's broken, you can see what you're getting into.

Loose mortise-and-tenons—take the joint apart, clean thoroughly and replace. If the fit is very loose, it can be wedged

wide as the end. Glue and tap in until tight. It enlarges the male end. It can also be done for a blind hole, but the wedge must be cut more carefully, with less waste material to be left inside the hole. **Chair-loc**—a chemical that causes the wood fibers to swell and stay enlarged permanently. Works well when the fit is not overly loose. It is especially useful for chair backs, spindles and delicate turnings where other types of repair would be ugly.

with wedges the same width as the tenon. If it is reasonably tight, casein glue will fill the space well enough, but resin glue will not. Do not use epoxy in a mortise because if the tenon breaks, it will be very difficult to remove the end.

Pinning a mortise and tenon joint—If the joint has a dowel pinning it together, remove it. If the pin goes through both sides of the wood, it can simply be driven out with a pin punch. If it only goes through one side of the mortise and the tenon, it must be pulled out. If it's loose, you can just drill a tiny hole in it, insert a

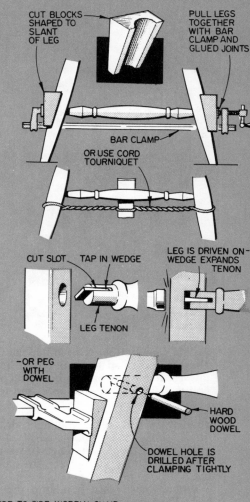

TIGHTENING LOOSE TURNED TENONS

CUT BLOCKS SHAPED TO SLANT OF LEG

PULL LEGS TOGETHER WITH BAR CLAMP AND GLUED JOINTS

BAR CLAMP

OR USE CORD TOURNIQUET

CUT SLOT   TAP IN WEDGE

LEG IS DRIVEN ON- WEDGE EXPANDS TENON

LEG TENON

-OR PEG WITH DOWEL

HARD WOOD DOWEL

DOWEL HOLE IS DRILLED AFTER CLAMPING TIGHTLY

TIGHTENING LOOSE TURNED TENONS

USE STEEL PIN OR HEADLESS NO. 16 NAIL

■ DRILL FOR PIN ACROSS LEG TENON

SAW PEGS FLUSH

■ DRIVE NARROW WEDGES INTO SEAT MORTISE AROUND LEG TENON

■ CUT AND FIT NEW WOOD PATCH INTO MORTISE

BORE HOLE TO TAKE LEG TENON

REMAINDER OF OLD HOLE

■ FILL OLD LOOSE MORTISE WITH EPOXY MIX

DRILL NEW HOLE TO FIT OLD LEG TENON

SIDE TO SIDE WOBBLY CHAIR

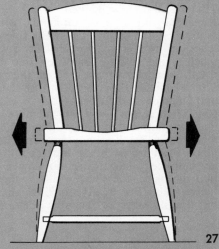

27

MEANS LOOSE JOINTS AS LEGS WORK AND FORCE THEIR SOCKETS OUT OF SHAPE

An old cane-bottom chair in bad condition. The cane seat had to be removed because the seat frame was broken in several places. Entire chair will be taken apart and rebuilt.

An antique plank seat chair that has been refinished with clear, natural materials to let the grain show. Although clear finishes are popular today, chair was painted brick red.

small screw and pull. If it is tight, drill the whole thing out, using a drill slightly smaller than the dowel. Then break away the remainder of the dowel with knife or awl.

When you replace it, clamp the joint first. Then re-drill the dowel hole, going up on size with the drill. Replace with the same size dowel, well glued.

Repairing a mortise—often a twisting motion on a chair will cause the side of a tenon to break away. Repair with a wood patch using a little more overlap than usual for added strength. Make the patch a little thicker than the depth of the cut and plane or sand flush.

Repairing a tenon—a much more frequent repair, but not too difficult if you work carefully. Cut any broken bits of tenon off flush with the butt end of the piece to be joined. Carefully saw a slot into the piece, the same width as the old tenon. You are really making an end mortise in that piece. Then you cut a dou-

ble tenon, fitting one end into the mortise of the piece that formerly had the tenon. And the other end of the tenon goes into the original mortise.

Clamping chairs—chair frames are usually irregular and difficult to clamp. But clamping is even more important for chairs than other type furniture, so do not neglect it. There are several tricks, like the windlass or tourniquet. When all the legs and rungs have been glued, place the chair on a flat, level surface (so it won't cure deformed), weight it down with books or something, and wrap three or four turns of soft rope around the leg ends. Insert a stick and twist until the rope is tight. Nothing else beats it.

The band clamp, which is a webb belt with a screw sinching mechanism, is a little easier to use, but it isn't much better for chairs. For irregular surfaces such as turned legs, use a sandbag or a fitted block with the clamps to prevent marring the surfaces.

The leg of this Windsor chair has come loose. Hole in the seat has become so enlarged that glue will not hold it very long. Hole is filled with epoxy and redrilled.

CORNER BRACES

Most chairs of the mortise-and-tenon type have corner braces or corner blocks to support the aprons and legs. There are several types, both of metal and wood, and they are usually held by glue and screws. They are very necessary to the strength of the chair and any that are missing, broken, split or loose must be replaced.

A wooden block that is simply loose can be used again, most likely. Turn out the screws, clean the glue surfaces thoroughly, and replace. If the screw threads have broken and the hole become enlarged, use a slightly larger screw if it will fit, or a slightly longer one. Be careful not to drive it out the other side.

If a block brace is missing, the easiest way to replace it is remove one of the others and copy it. Then replace both. Blocks should be at least 1½″ thick with the grain running diagonally across the corner. Pre-drill them to prevent splitting.

If the chair has a metal brace, it is less likely to become broken, but if it should, it must be replaced. Perhaps you can find a similar brace on a chair in a junk shop somewhere, but that's a lot of work for

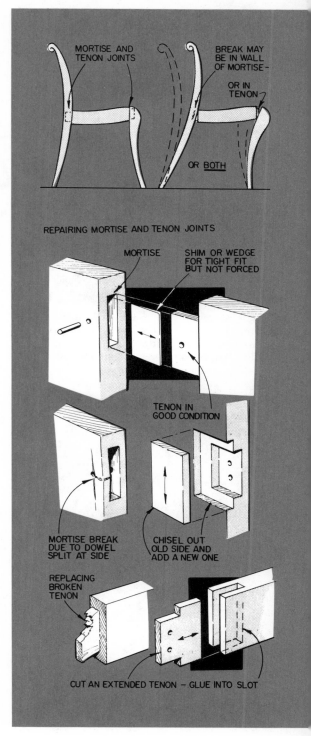

MORTISE AND TENON JOINTS

BREAK MAY BE IN WALL OF MORTISE—

OR IN TENON

OR BOTH

REPAIRING MORTISE AND TENON JOINTS

MORTISE

SHIM OR WEDGE FOR TIGHT FIT BUT NOT FORCED

TENON IN GOOD CONDITION

MORTISE BREAK DUE TO DOWEL SPLIT AT SIDE

CHISEL OUT OLD SIDE AND ADD A NEW ONE

REPLACING BROKEN TENON

CUT AN EXTENDED TENON – GLUE INTO SLOT

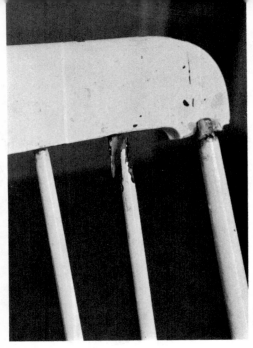

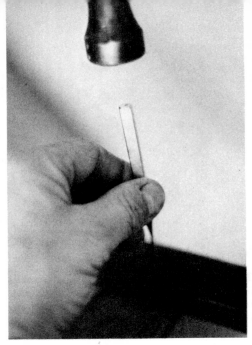

The round mortise in the back of this rocking chair has broken away so turned end will no longer hold. As a result, back spindles have also broken. Make a wood patch.

A pin punch is invaluable for removing tiny brads and nails often used to hold mortise and tenon joints together. Larger diameter pin punches are used to remove dowels.

Chair rungs being glued under pressure from a tourniquet. Protect finish with pads where rope touches the legs. Keep chair level until glue sets to prevent warping.

such a small gain. Just make a wooden brace to replace the metal one, but be sure the block covers slots in the apron and that screw holes do not hit them.

SPLIT RUNGS AND SPINDLES

Sometimes a chair part will split, rather than break. Repair is simple enough—just glue and clamp. The problem is that if the grain is angled to produce a long split once, it will often happen again. And again. Also, the wood that has become weakened will re-split. By all means reglue it several times before resorting to more drastic measures. Sometimes only three or four of the grain lines cross the spindle and when they've been glued, the piece will be stronger than it was originally. For gluing splits, use resin glue.

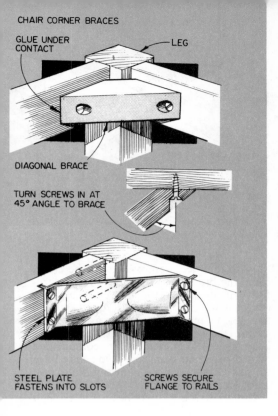

CHAIR CORNER BRACES

GLUE UNDER CONTACT

LEG

DIAGONAL BRACE

TURN SCREWS IN AT 45° ANGLE TO BRACE

STEEL PLATE FASTENS INTO SLOTS

SCREWS SECURE FLANGE TO RAILS

Leg of an old table is joined to aprons by mortise and tenon joints and reinforced later by glued blocks. To remove top, simply turn out screws inlet into aprons at an angle.

Chair spindle has broken in long clean scarf so it will be easy to repair. Make a trial fitting before applying glue to make sure the wood fibers will line up and fit properly.

WOOD SPLINTS AND PATCHES

A break that is more than a split must be patched by other methods. Namely the splint. It is merely two pieces of the same kind of wood as the broken piece mortised in to lap the break and shaped to the original contours. It sounds easy and it can be, but the work must be done carefully. This is no place for large carpenter's tools.

In the case of a broken spindle or bow back, for example, a break frequently occurs near the holes for dowels, tenons, etc. Before attempting repairs, take the entire broken piece off, if possible. If other joints are tight, they can usually be loosened by knocking out any pins or dowels holding them and gently tapping apart with soft-faced mallet.

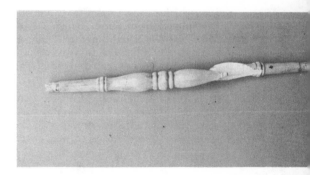

Apply glue to both faces of the break. Plastic resin glue is best for this kind of job since it will make the joint stronger than the rest of wood. For bad fitting breaks, use casein.

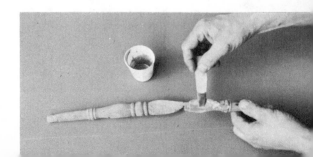

Broken spindle is held under pressure of C-clamp while glue dries. Glue will set faster if heat is applied to joint. On softer woods, use blocks or pads to protect from marks.

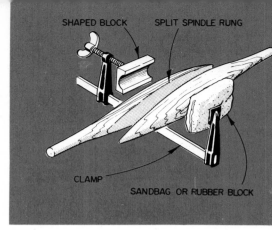

SHAPED BLOCK   SPLIT SPINDLE RUNG

CLAMP

SANDBAG OR RUBBER BLOCK

The other spindle from same chair has bad break and cannot be fitted together again. A splint-like patch will have to be used to lap the broken spot. Results can be excellent.

First step is to cut away rabbet for patch on both sides of the break. Longitudinal surfaces must line up perfectly or the spindle will end up being crooked. Align with rasp.

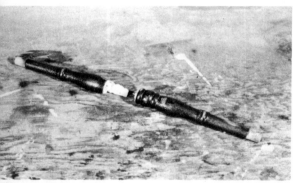

With the piece removed from the chair, clean the broken ends, glue well and carefully fit the ends together just as they came apart. Tap the ends together until the seam line is as small as possible. Clamp the broken piece to workbench to keep it in alignment. For complicated turned or steam bent parts, you may have to make a jig to hold it firmly while you work on it.

Cut two wooden patches large enough to lap the break by at least 1½ times the thickness of the piece at the break. Thus, if it is 1″ thick at the break, the patch should overlap 1½″ on each side making it 3″ long overall. The patch should be thick enough so it can be shaped to the original contours of the piece. It should also be of the same kind of wood, of course, with grain running across the break.

With a scriber, mark the outlines of the patch precisely. Using a very fine saw, cut out a rabbet into which the patch is recessed. In the case of turned parts, this is simply a cross cut. Use a small, very sharp chisel to remove the wood to a depth of ¼ the thickness of the piece. Make a similar recess on the other side. Then fit the patches in with lots of glue and clamp. After pressure is applied, scour out the tenon hole to remove any glue extruded into it.

After the glue has set thoroughly (usually 24 hours), remove the clamps and shape the patches to the form of the piece. For this, a spokeshave and woodworkers riffler file set are handy. End up with very fine sandpaper and apply finish

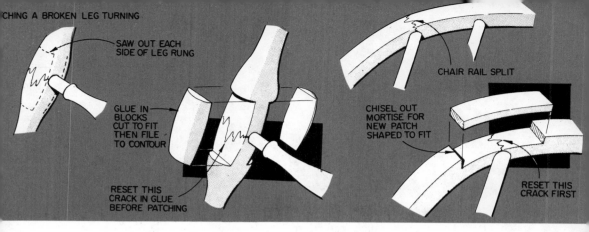

SAW OUT EACH SIDE OF LEG RUNG

GLUE IN BLOCKS CUT TO FIT THEN FILE TO CONTOUR

RESET THIS CRACK IN GLUE BEFORE PATCHING

CHAIR RAIL SPLIT

CHISEL OUT MORTISE FOR NEW PATCH SHAPED TO FIT

RESET THIS CRACK FIRST

to match the old. For small patches, you can often amalgamate the old finish over the patched area. This is simply softening the existing finish and spreading it out to cover.

Things to remember are: cut the patches before cutting the mortises to receive them; make the fit quite snug; use same wood and grain if possible; use plenty of glue; don't be afraid to make the patch a little "fat" if necessary for strength; and amalgamate the old finish over the patched area if possible.

IRREPARABLE AND MISSING PARTS

Sometimes you just can't fix it. The wood may be crushed or badly splintered, or the broken off piece missing. So you replace it. If it's a common "antique", meaning a commercial chair over 50 years old, you can probably cannibalize parts from other junk chairs. Spindles, especially, can be tailored to fit other chairs.

For turned parts such as legs and rungs, you may have to get them made. Take one of the other legs or rungs to the shop for a pattern. Square parts, you can generally make yourself if you are careful. Steam-bent parts, however, are generally beyond the capability and equipment of the home repairman. A bow back on a Windsor chair requires a very good cabinetmaker to replace, for example.

One half of the spindle has been glued and clamped. Now the other half is glued and clamped so that the spindle is aligned perfectly. Otherwise it won't fit back on chair.

Patch block is in place bridging the break like a splint. When glue is completely dry, clamps will be removed and the block carefully carved to contours of the spindle.

Wood rasp is used to do fine shaping of the patch after it has been rough carved to approximate shape. Different shaped rasps, coarse files, are used to get into tight spots.

Patch is sanded smooth after shaping is completed. By rotating spindle and holding sandpaper stationary the patch can be "turned" to almost exact diameter as the spindle.

Finished patch on broken spindle can now be stained to match rest of the finish. If the spindle is patched straight, the patch can be turned on wood lathe for perfect match.

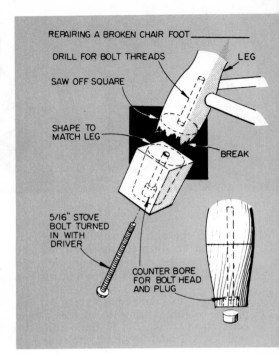

REPAIRING A BROKEN CHAIR FOOT

DRILL FOR BOLT THREADS — LEG

SAW OFF SQUARE

SHAPE TO MATCH LEG

BREAK

5/16" STOVE BOLT TURNED IN WITH DRIVER

COUNTER BORE FOR BOLT HEAD AND PLUG

BROKEN CHAIR FOOT

A chair leg that is short by virtue of wear or a break can be fixed rather easily. First, cut off the ragged end of the leg squarely with a fine cut saw. Make a new end of hard wood, only approximately shaped and a little longer than the final leg must be. Drill a ¼" hole through the center of the wood blank and into the center of the short leg end. Countersink the hold in the blank to a depth equalling at least ¼" inside the final cut-off mark if you wish to use a steel dowel pin or a stove bolt. Plug with dowel. If you use a wooden dowel instead of a bolt, make the hole half as large as the minimum diameter of the leg.

Perhaps the easiest and strongest pin is a ¼" flat head stove bolt. Cover well with epoxy glue, including the inside of the hole, and turn in like a screw until it pulls the block tight against the leg. Do not turn too hard because the wood "threads" will pull loose. After the glue is thoroughly cured, cut the new foot off to make the chair level. Shape the patch and finish as described above.

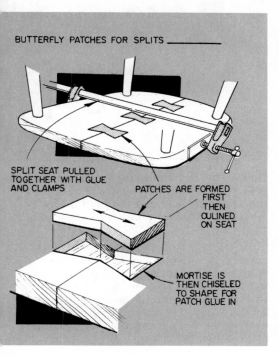

BUTTERFLY PATCHES FOR SPLITS _____

SPLIT SEAT PULLED
TOGETHER WITH GLUE
AND CLAMPS

PATCHES ARE FORMED
FIRST
THEN
OUTLINED
ON SEAT

MORTISE IS
THEN CHISELED
TO SHAPE FOR
PATCH GLUE IN

PLANK SEAT SPLITS

A solid plank seat such as you find on
Windsor chairs is called a plank seat.
They are amazingly rugged but once in a
while one splits, usually the result of terrible abuse.

Repairing a plank seat is not difficult,
but it must be a rugged repair since it is
the foundation of that type chair.

Perhaps the easiest way to put the two
halves together again securely is with a
patented device called a Tite-Joint Fastener. It amounts to a bolt with a round
nut on one end. Drill into the edges of the
split as if installing a dowel, with both
lined up exactly. Then bore a larger hole
across these edge holes from the bottom
of the seat. They should be no deeper
than the edge-hole plus 1/16th inch or
so. Install the special bolt as if it were a
dowel. Drop a metal ring into the hole
with the threaded end of the bolt. This
acts as a washer. Place the spherical nut
inside the ring washer and turn the bolt
into it to hold. Then put the other end of
the bolt in the edge hole of the other side
of the seat until the end appears in that

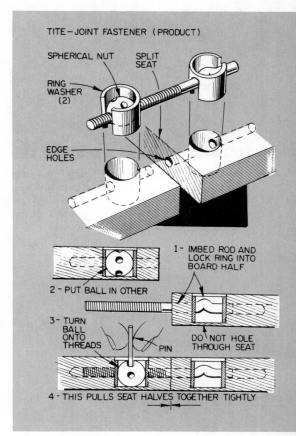

TITE—JOINT FASTENER (PRODUCT)

SPHERICAL NUT   SPLIT
SEAT
RING
WASHER
(2)

EDGE
HOLES

1 - IMBED ROD AND
LOCK RING INTO
BOARD HALF

2 - PUT BALL IN OTHER

3 - TURN
BALL
ONTO
THREADS   PIN

DO NOT HOLE
THROUGH SEAT

4 - THIS PULLS SEAT HALVES TOGETHER TIGHTLY

**Wood patch is the plank seat of an antique
chair. This patch is so old it was held by
three square cut nails but remained intact
over years because it was so perfectly fitted.**

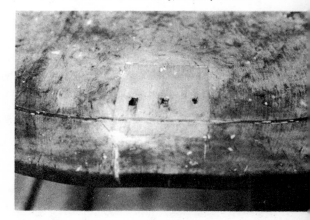

Dowelling jig guides electric drill into edge of board which is to be edge glued. If dowel holes do not line up perfectly, the surfaces of boards will have to be planed down.

Dowel hole is countersunk to make a glue well. Otherwise excess glue will be forced out under pressure and not hold dowel as well. Under pressure, glue is forced into hole.

Dowel inserted in edge of board, ready for gluing. The scratch line marks center of board so they will align perfectly. If not, dowel can be shaved down or hole drilled.

Both edges that meet are glued with plastic resin glue. If there are gaps and edges do not fit very well, use casein glue. It fills better. Wipe off glue as pressure is applied.

cross hole. Drop another special ring washer over it to hold it in place. Then use a nail in the holes in the spherical nut to turn it until the edges are drawn together tightly. Use three Tite-Joint Fasteners for an average seat bottom. Glue liberally before tightening.

THE BUTTERFLY PATCH

While the Tite-Joint Fastener is fairly easy, it does cost money and the presence of ugly metal fasteners in an antique can ruin it's value. What the dealers like to see are well made butterfly patches. It is actually, just a double dovetail insert patch, installed across the split. Make three to six butterfly shaped patches of hardwood. They should be 2½″ to 4″ long, 1½″ to 1″ wide at the outside and at least ¼″ thick. The sides should be square.

Next, glue and clamp the seat bottom, cleaning the edges as usual to make sure the glue holds. While the seat in is clamps, locate the butterfly patches along the crack and scribe the outlines. Cut a mortise for each just a trifle less deep than the thickness of the patch. Make the bottoms of the mortises flat so they will make complete contact with the faces of the patches. Using glue and pressure, install the butterfly patches. When all glue has completely cured, remove clamps, plane patches flush and refinish them if desired. It's a secure patch and it adds a

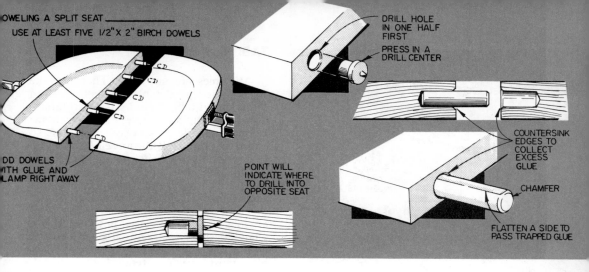

lot of character to a busted old piece of furniture.

The butterfly patch is also used for table tops, bureau tops and any long splits.

DOWELS

Dowels are a cheap and effective way to fix a split seat, or indeed to join any boards along their edges. The problem with a seat split is getting the dowel holes lined up exactly. Unlike raw lumber which can be planed flush after joining, a chair seat must line up perfectly on each side of the split. And when the dowel holes don't line up, the top faces won't line up.

If the split is reasonably square, the problem is somewhat simpler. But where it is ragged or at an angle, you must work slowly and carefully. After cleaning the edge, drill holes along one edge for dowels. These holes should be parallel to the bottom face of the seat and to the edge of the seat that is at right angles to the split, more or less. There are several commercial doweling jigs to help you do it, but they also require great care in using.

Then place dowel centers in each hole. These are little plugs with a point and are quite inexpensive at hardware stores. Place the two halves of the chair seat on a flat surface and press the split edges together. The dowel center points will mark the location of holes on the opposite edge.

If the chair is assembled except for the split, it will not be possible to place the seat on a flat surface. Instead use two 2x4s underneath, with their ends resting on saw horses and shimmed until they are exactly parallel. Then press the split edges together as described above.

Once the locations are marked, drill the dowel holes in the opposite edge, taking care that they are parallel to the bottom face and to the edge at right angles to the split. That's the only way to make the holes line up perfectly.

Insert the dowels for a trial fit and press the edges together tightly. If the top and bottom faces of the seat do not match, you will have to change the dowels or the holes to compensate. Perhaps it's easiest to rout out the hole on the side next to the high face. Then, before assembling permanently, fill the voids in the dowel hole with epoxy. An alternate way to make surfaces flush is to shave a little off the dowel on the high side.

When you have adjusted the dowels and holes to make the faces of the seat line up as well as possible, coat dowels and edges with resin glue and clamp tightly. The bond, when cured, will be stronger than the wood itself.

Note that dowels should be grooved so glue will flow around them. Ends should be chamfered and the holes deeper than the length of the dowels and should be countersunk to make reservoirs for glue forced out by the clamping.

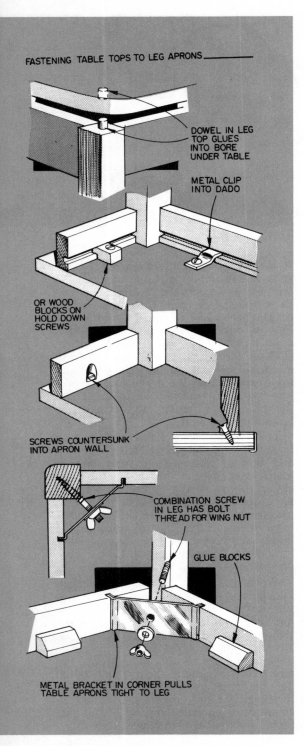

FASTENING TABLE TOPS TO LEG APRONS

DOWEL IN LEG TOP GLUES INTO BORE UNDER TABLE

METAL CLIP INTO DADO

OR WOOD BLOCKS ON HOLD DOWN SCREWS

SCREWS COUNTERSUNK INTO APRON WALL

COMBINATION SCREW IN LEG HAS BOLT THREAD FOR WING NUT

GLUE BLOCKS

METAL BRACKET IN CORNER PULLS TABLE APRONS TIGHT TO LEG

TABLES

All tables are not alike. There are the trusty four-legged tables, of course. And three-legged tables. And six-legged tables. There are trestle tables and sawhorse campaign tables. And other tables so weird they don't fall into any category.

Every table has its unique problems, but they all have much more in common. For broken legs and stretchers, use the same repair techniques described under the previous section on chairs. The most obvious thing a table has, however, that a chair doesn't is a large flat board known as the top. It is heir to all sorts of troubles, most of which require it's removal.

HOW TO GET THE TABLE TOP OFF

If the top is warped, split or broken, it should certainly be removed before you try to work on it. And many people find it easier to refinish when it is off the frame and legs. And if the legs or aprons need work, you can get at them easier with the top off.

Getting the top iff is easy. Usually, you can see how to do it just by turning the table over. The usual systems are glue blocks, wooden fasteners with screws, metal fasteners with screws, recessed screws in the aprons and the corner bracket with wing nut. In all cases except the first and last, simply turn out all the screws and the top will usually come free of the frame. In the case of corner brackets, usually found in more modern dining tables, there is a hanger bolt in the leg itself, at a 45° angle so it slips through the center hole in the corner bracket where it is tightened with a wing nut. If the leg is loose, a turn or two will tighten it. And when you want to remove the legs, take the wing nuts off and the legs come free. The aprons are still attached to the top, however. They may be removed by one of the other methods, depending on how they are fastened.

A common method formerly used for fastening apron and top are glue blocks. Sometimes these are also held by screws. If so, remove them and whack the ends of the blocks sharply with a hammer. They will pop loose. Unless they split, they can be reused, after cleaning off all glue, of course. Those that break can be replaced.

Sometimes a top will be held by dowels. They may be in the aprons, but usually are found in the top of the legs. The trouble is that you can't see them. They are often used in conjunction with other fasteners, so if you remove every one in sight and the top still won't come free, it may be dowels. Gently tap the top with a soft-faced mallet to loosen the dowels. But take it easy. Tops split rather easily.

Some old or antique table tops may be held by tapered dowels driven in from above, probably into the leg ends. In most cases, they can be loosened and removed by tapping from underneath near the dowel. As always, take it easy. If that doesn't do it, drill out the dowel using a drill about 2/3rds the size of the dowel. Then cave in the sides of the dowel with a knife blade or small chisel.

If a top is held down by nails driven from either top or bottom, you can be almost sure they were the result of some misguided attempt at repair. Carefully remove them and discard. Reattach the top by the method most likely to have been used originally.

SPLIT TOPS

In general, a split top should be treated in the same way as a plank seat split, described on page 35. However a table top is longer, wider and thinner than a chair seat and usually has a highly polished finish so there are important differences. For example, you couldn't use a patented Tite-Joint fastener on a thin table top. But a couple of dowels or butterfly patches may be called for.

It is almost always easiest to remove a split table top completely before trying to mend it. Or remove the drop leaf only, if the rest of the top is sound.

A distinction should be made between complete splits (when the top is in two pieces) and a partial split. Often a partial split is easiest to fix if you split it all the way. That way, surfaces can be cleaned and lined up better.

For mending a partial split, first clean out every bit of dirt, wax, oil and gunk

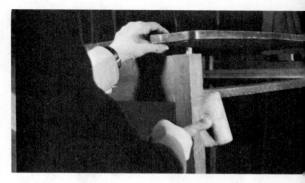

Table top can be removed by slight tapping with wooden or soft faced mallet. Make sure all screws and nails through apron on underside have been removed or tapping splinters.

Table leg of newer dining tables can be easily removed just be unscrewing nut from the hanger bolt. A tap or two and the leg comes off. Older tables are more complicated.

Glue blocks are often used to hold table top to aprons. They are easily removed by giving them each a sharp blow with a hammer. They pop right off without harming either.

The drop leaf of a table which has split being reglued. Furniture clamps are blocked to keep edge from being marred. Slight curving of the board is warping from age.

Steel square shows up the slight warping of the drop leaf of an antique table. Most collectors think a small amount of warping adds charm and authenticity to antiques.

that has worked its way in. Before gluing, it is a good idea to draw the split together slowly with clamps to make certain they line up perfectly. Especially when the split is splintery, wood fibers can lodge crossways in the split and prevent a perfect fit. Release the clamps and apply resin glue to both sides of the crack. Use a string or thread to work the glue well back into the apex of the split. Then apply clamps again, wiping away glue that is extruded with the pressure. If there is any danger of the clamps causing the top to set with a bow or warp, put boards across the grain and clamp the ends to hold the top flat.

If the top is split into two pieces, the procedure is the same except that you will find it easier to clean and apply glue. In some cases, the wood may be rotted or so dry and brittle it splinters badly and cannot be successfully reglued. If the faulty wood includes most of the top, it may be best just to make an entirely new top. If the faulty wood is along the grain for most of the length, of the top but does not cover much of the width, saw out the bad wood and replace it with a strip of matching good wood. The replacement wood should be the same kind, of course, and with the same grain figure and color, too, if possible. You will probably have to strip off the old finish before trying to match color. It is important to keep the dimensions of the top, after repairs, the same as it was originally. Otherwise the fasteners will not line up.

WARPED TOPS

Antique dealers and owners of rare 300-year-old furniture pieces say that a little warp in a table top makes it more valuable. There's something interesting about an old board that's slightly twisted. They say. But maybe that's because there is almost nothing you can do about a warped top. Nothing that will be permanent, anyway.

There are two causes of warping: a difference in moisture content within the board, and changes in the chemical structure within the board. In each case, the size of the fibers in the wood are changed more in one place than another, resulting in a curving.

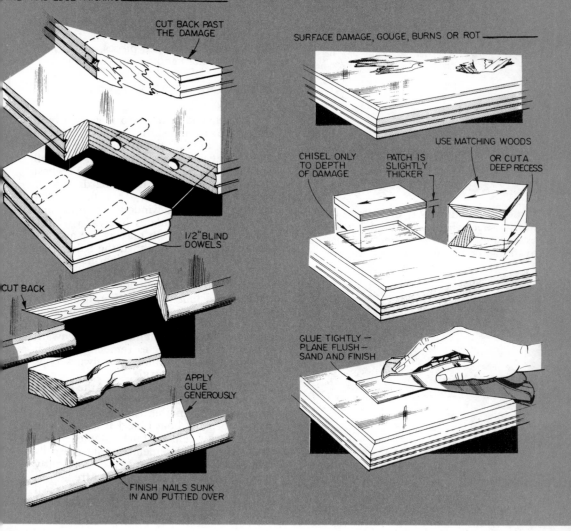

CUT BACK PAST THE DAMAGE

SURFACE DAMAGE, GOUGE, BURNS OR ROT

1/2" BLIND DOWELS

CUT BACK

APPLY GLUE GENEROUSLY

FINISH NAILS SUNK IN AND PUTTIED OVER

CHISEL ONLY TO DEPTH OF DAMAGE

PATCH IS SLIGHTLY THICKER

USE MATCHING WOODS

OR CUT A DEEP RECESS

GLUE TIGHTLY — PLANE FLUSH — SAND AND FINISH

When a board is warped because of chemical changes, there is almost nothing you can do, short of rather drastic measures which will be described a little further on. What happens is that the resins in the wood oxidize. This causes the molecules to link up and take up less space. And so the wood contracts where the oxidation took place. If the other side of the board does not oxidize equally, as often happens when one side of a top is finished and the other is not, the board will warp, curving inward on the unfinished side.

Warping caused by chemical changes cannot be completely corrected without sawing the boards apart and regluing them. However, you can stop the chemical action by finishing *both* sides. This prevents unequal oxidization. In the case of valuable antique furniture, you would decrease its value by finishing the underside of the table top, however. The unfinished side is one of the signs that collectors look for when trying judge authenticity and age of a piece. If that is your case, seal the unfinished side with paste wax or boiled linseed oil. It will have to be re-

Underside of drop leaf of antique table is not finished which permits moisture to be evaporated from wood fibers causing them to shrink. Board curves toward the dry side.

One way to help reduce a curved warp is to restore moisture to the dried out side and to dry out the finished side, thus equalizing the moisture content between the two sides.

When board has been made reasonably flat and unwarped by wetting and drying, apply a sealer coat to the unfinished side to prevent further drying out, especially in winter.

newed from time to time. If the top is very old or badly warped, it is too late, but for slightly warped pieces, it will help prevent further bending and twisting.

HEAT AND WATER TREATMENT

The other kind of warp is caused by a difference in moisture content between one side of the board and the other. Moisture causes the wood fibers to swell and heat causes them to shrink. The best example of this is the floor boards in your house. In the summer, they fit together tightly because the windows are open and the humid air circulates freely. In winter, the furnace comes on making the average American house drier than the Sahara desert (literally) so the boards shrink.

The same thing happens with your furniture. And if a table top is not sealed with a good finish on one side, it may absorb moisture in the summer and become super dry in winter, causing it to warp slightly upward in summer and downward in winter. The point to remember is that a warp caused by moisture always cups away from the moist side.

The cure is simple. Dry out the convex side of the board and/or dampen the concave side. When this is done sufficiently to un-warp the board, seal it as best you can. It may remain fairly stable. However, you should remember that the cells that make up a board are constantly working and they have enough strength to overcome any measures you can take. All you do by sealing is to keep the cell working down to a minimum.

ANNULAR RING WARPAGE

This is where warping gets complicated and fancy. Because a board will warp and twist into strange shapes because of the configuration of the grain and particularly the hard annular rings. Even though there be no difference in moisture content between one side of a board and the other, the effect of shrinkage will be different on the grain on one side than it is on the other. To understand this, look at the end of a board that has been cut with the sides parallel to the radius of the trunk of the tree. This is called a radial cut. The

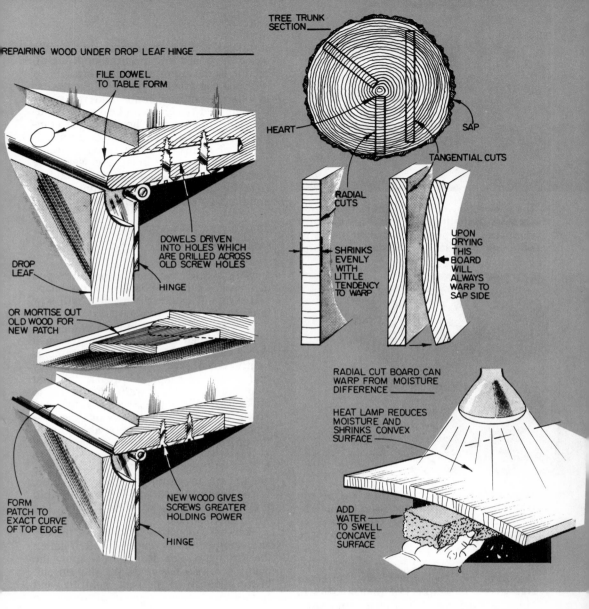

REPAIRING WOOD UNDER DROP LEAF HINGE

FILE DOWEL TO TABLE FORM

HEART

SAP

TANGENTIAL CUTS

DOWELS DRIVEN INTO HOLES WHICH ARE DRILLED ACROSS OLD SCREW HOLES

DROP LEAF

HINGE

RADIAL CUTS

SHRINKS EVENLY WITH LITTLE TENDENCY TO WARP

UPON DRYING THIS BOARD WILL ALWAYS WARP TO SAP SIDE

OR MORTISE OUT OLD WOOD FOR NEW PATCH

RADIAL CUT BOARD CAN WARP FROM MOISTURE DIFFERENCE

HEAT LAMP REDUCES MOISTURE AND SHRINKS CONVEX SURFACE

FORM PATCH TO EXACT CURVE OF TOP EDGE

NEW WOOD GIVES SCREWS GREATER HOLDING POWER

HINGE

ADD WATER TO SWELL CONCAVE SURFACE

rings appear in the board as almost straight lines running parallel across the board. As the fibers in a radial cut board shrink, the contraction is even and there is little warpage, so long as the moisture content is even throughout.

But look at a board with sides cut perpendicular to the radius of the tree trunk. This is called a tangential cut. The annular rings run lenghwise across the end of the board and curve noticeably. As the

board dries, the shrinkage of the rings is always greater than the shrinkage of the fibers between the rings. If the trunk is large enough and the board cut far enough out in the log, the rings will be almost parallel and run the length of the cross-section of the board. Shrinkage will be more even and warpage less. But when the rings are curved to a tighter radius and cross the board at the ends of the cross section, but terminate on the same side of the board near the center, the

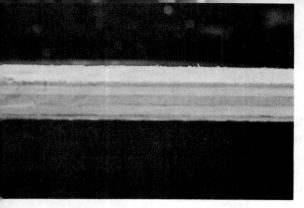

The reason plywood does not warp is easily seen in this edge-on view. The grain of alternate wood plies runs at right angles to adjoining one, to stop tendency to warp.

Large, relatively thin table tops like this old trestle table are prevented from warping by a "breadboard" end. The cross board are rabbeted for the long boards to fit into them.

Warping can be temporarily corrected sometimes by simply clamping as shown. There is danger that bad warps may split. Unless board is sealed, warp will return.

shrinkage will be very uneven and usually cause the board to cup in the opposite direction as the curvature of the rings.

When the grain is very complicates, as in boards cut near limbs and roots, the warping and twisting can be very complicated. In other cases, however, the complications of the grain produces a nutralization of shrinkage effects such as found in burl. Plywood is relatively warp free because the grain of each ply is laid at right angles to the next, cancelling out the annular ring warpage throughout.

REMOVING WARPS MECHANICALLY

With enough mechanical pressure, you can always force a board into any shape you want. That doesn't mean it will stay in that shape, however.

A warped table top, for example, can be straightened somewhat by fastening it down tighter. But if the table frame is lightly constructed the top may simply pull it out of shape. However, the first step in removing a warp should be to make sure the top is securely fastened down. If glue blocks, screws or other fasteners are loose, you may be able to cure the problem by just tightening them.

If that fails, remove the top and clamp it flat, using the heat-and-moisture method of un-warping at the same time. If the warp is great or the wood is old and brittle, go easy with the clamps. The wood may splinter.

Pairs of 2x4 across the grain of the top and clamped on the ends will often flatten the top again. For deep warps, apply the clamp screws a few turns per day on old, brittle boards to prevent splitting and splintering. At any sign of distress, stop and remove the clamps.

UN-WARPING WITH A SAW

This is a dangerous business because it can ruin a fine piece of furniture. But it can also produce amazing results in correcting the "uncorrectable" warp.

One method is to cut deep kerfs in the underside of the table top with a power saw. It obviously must be done in areas

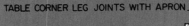
TABLE CORNER LEG JOINTS WITH APRON

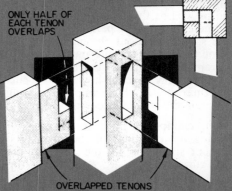

ONLY HALF OF
EACH TENON
OVERLAPS

OVERLAPPED TENONS

TYPICAL TABLE WITH APRON AND LEG JOINTS

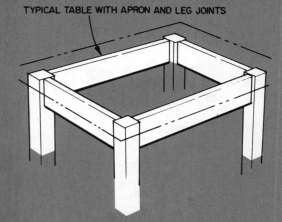

DRILL TO
TAKE DOWELS

DOWEL AND
TENON JOINT

TENON GOES
IN FIRST

MITERED TENONS

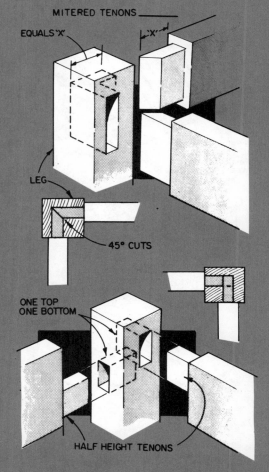

EQUALS 'X'

'X'

LEG

45° CUTS

ONE TOP
ONE BOTTOM

HALF HEIGHT TENONS

LOCKED DOWELS JOINT

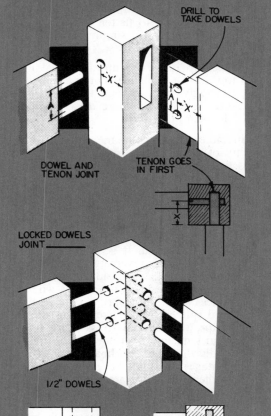

1/2" DOWELS

45

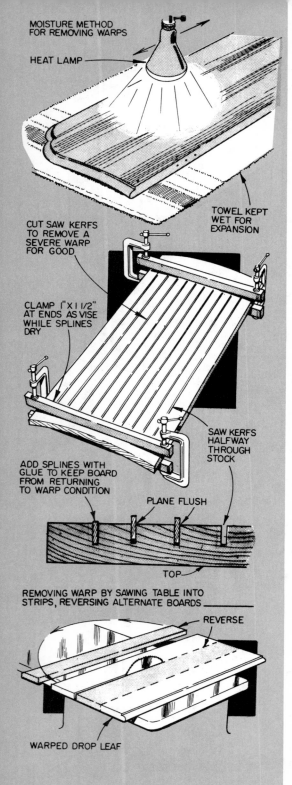

MOISTURE METHOD FOR REMOVING WARPS

HEAT LAMP

TOWEL KEPT WET FOR EXPANSION

CUT SAW KERFS TO REMOVE A SEVERE WARP FOR GOOD

CLAMP 1" X 1 1/2" AT ENDS AS VISE WHILE SPLINES DRY

SAW KERFS HALFWAY THROUGH STOCK

ADD SPLINES WITH GLUE TO KEEP BOARD FROM RETURNING TO WARP CONDITION

PLANE FLUSH

TOP

REMOVING WARP BY SAWING TABLE INTO STRIPS, REVERSING ALTERNATE BOARDS

REVERSE

WARPED DROP LEAF

that do not show, so it isn't proper for a drop leaf. Before removing the top from the table, mark where all fasteners are located as well as the areas that are visible. Then make a series of parallel cuts with a power saw, each about one-half the thickness of the top. The cuts must run with the grain but not go to the edges of the top where they would show. Make cuts about three or four inches apart, keeping well within the area marked.

Then clamp the top flat, keeping all clamping devices clear of the saw kerfs. Next, cut splines to fill the kerfs. If the top is curved downward (that is the top surface is convex), make the splines a little wider than the kerfs and plane to a slightly wedged cross section. When you tap the wedges spline into the kerfs, the pressure will tend to flatten the top. But too much tapping will simply reverse the warp.

If the top is curved upward (making the top surface concave) cut the splines to fit snugly but without the wedging pressure. It must act more as a filler to hold the board flat.

In either case, insert the splines with plenty of casein glue, wipe clean the excess and allow to cure completely before removing the clamps. Sand the splines flush and apply a sealer to hold the moisture content constant before removing the clamps.

Another method of correcting a warp is even more radical. It is simply sawing the top into strips, reversing every other one, and regluing. The advantages are that for drop leaves and other tops where both sides show, there are no unsightly kerfs and splines. And by reversing alternate strips, the internal stresses are reversed and tend to cancel one another out, supposedly holding the board flat. The disadvantages are that the grain may not match where the strips are glued, and the total width of the top will be reduced by the sum of the width of the saw cuts. On a drop leaf, this won't matter much but for a top that is held by screws, the holes would no longer line up. And if the top fits the table frame snugly, the sawing proceedure may make it impossible to replace.

Radical surgery can cure bad warping. Grooves are scored in underside of warped top, in areas where they wont' show. Then wood splines are inserted, glued, and planed off smooth.

Wood splines are driven into grooves and glued. If top warps toward grooves, wedge out by making splines a little "fat". For opposite warp, make splines fit looser and clamp flat.

Wood patch fits neatly into top of pine chest although other blemishes were never repaired. Wood grain matches, and due to skillful staining, color also matches well.

Knot in this antique table top was originally sealed and finished over but has dried out over the years and worked loose so it will have to be re-filled or patched as indicated.

TOP INSERTS AND PATCHES

If a split break or rotten wood ruins a considerable area of the table top, the whole section should be removed and a new piece inserted. Measure the length and width exactly. Cut the top in straight lines through the good wood but as close as possible to the ruined wood. Replace it with a new piece.

The insert piece should be of the same type wood, of course, and match in color and grain if possible. It should be the exact width of the piece removed so the dimensions of the top do not change. And it should be slightly thicker, so it can be planed flush, top and bottom. Then the entire top must be sanded to bare wood and refinished.

When a top is broken, either at a corner or along an edge, it must be patched with the same type wood. Again, it should be slightly thicker than the thickness of the table top. Cut the patch first, to cover the ruined area. Then carefully scribe around the patch on the top and even more carefully cut away the ruined part with a fine-toothed saw. If the patch is large and there is likely to be much pressure on it, it can be blind doweled. And/or dovetailed.

LOOSE HINGES

When screw threads strip, you can often replace them with a size longer and they will hold tightly. It isn't often that you can use a size larger screw, however, because hinges and hardware are drilled and countersunk for a particular screw size. If the hardware isn't a valuable antique, you can bore and ream the holes to fit a larger size screw. But don't try it on tables even suspected of being antiques because it would reduce its value.

Another way to make screws hold is with glue, putty or expanders. Epoxy putty will hold very tightly, in fact almost permanently. This can be a disadvantage if the wood is old and brittle because the epoxy may just pull away a large chunk, leaving you with the problem of patching and getting the old epoxy off of the screw so you can reuse the hinge. The cellulose compounds commonly called "plastic wood" hold pretty well but not as well as epoxy.

Where wood is brittle or rotted, the trick is to provide something solid for the screws to sink into. Dowels work well. Just drill into the edge of the top so the dowel hole crosses the screw holes. Go about an inch beyond the farthest screw hole. Then insert dowels with lots of glue. When dry, shape the ends to the contour of the table edge, bore pilot holes in the old screw holes so the screws will not split the dowels. Then replace hinge where it was originally.

Another way to accomplish the same

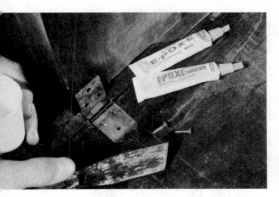

Hinge screws have worked loose in this old drop leaf. Holes are being filled with epoxy putty which will then be re-drilled. Larger size screws won't fit through hinge holes.

Patches over patches were utilized to repair damage done when this desk hinge broke away from desk top. Screws through last patch cured problem but are unsightly.

thing as dowels is by making a patch which covers the entire area of the hinge plate, plus at least 1½″ on either side. Mortise the patch in carefully, glue with plastic resin glue and clamp. Shape and finish the patch when the glue is thoroughly set and drill new pilot holes for the screws. Then simply put the hinge back where it was originally.

VENEER TOP PROBLEMS

Most of them consist of loose veneer, and if that's all that's wrong, the top usually does not have to be removed. Simply inject glue under the loose area, drilling a small hole if necessary, and clamp. Be sure to cover the top with wax paper or even heavy newspaper, so the clamp board won't be permanently affixed to the top. The paper can be scraped, soaked or sanded away easily.

When veneer is missing, you either patch or replace it. See general description of veneer patching on page 24.

FIXING LEGS, STRETCHERS AND RAILS

The cure for loose and wobbly legs depends on the type of table. There is quite a difference. A typical dinner table which expands for leaves has legs that are held each by a single bolt. There will be either

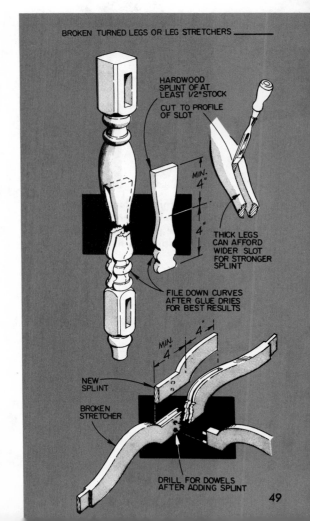

BROKEN TURNED LEGS OR LEG STRETCHERS _____

HARDWOOD SPLINT OF AT LEAST 1/2" STOCK

CUT TO PROFILE OF SLOT

MIN. 4"

4"

THICK LEGS CAN AFFORD WIDER SLOT FOR STRONGER SPLINT

FILE DOWN CURVES AFTER GLUE DRIES FOR BEST RESULTS

MIN. 4"

4"

NEW SPLINT

BROKEN STRETCHER

DRILL FOR DOWELS AFTER ADDING SPLINT

Wedged joint holds the stretcher to the trestle of this harvest table. Beauty of such joints is that they can be tightened by tapping wedges or removed to take table apart.

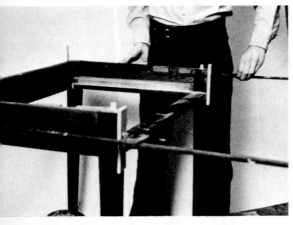

Table frame in furniture clamps. The mortise and tenon joints have been cleaned and reglued to make the piece stronger than ever. Gluing must be done on flat, level surface.

a metal or wooden diagonal brace across the apron corners with the leg bolt in it. Tighten the nuts and the legs are tight. You have to do this frequently, though, because the table is moved so much getting the leaves in and out.

Older tables (and better ones) have the aprons joined to the legs by mortises and tenons. They were originally fitted with very close tolerances but they may have become loose by "working". They may have been glued or pinned with a small dowel, or both. Both of these may have loosened over the years.

Remove the top and check the four legs for looseness. If two or more are loose, disassemble the entire table frame. Wooden pins can be driven out with a pin punch. For those that do not go through, pull them out by drilling a small hole in the end of the pin, inserting an appropriate sized eye screw and pulling. If that won't get it, drill out the pin with a drill slightly smaller than the pin and carefully cave in the remainder of the pin with an awl or ice pick.

When the wooden pins are removed, carefully pull the legs away from the aprons, exercising care not to break the tenons. You may have to use a soft faced mallet, but go easy. Remember which piece goes where, even if you have to write it out on masking tape stuck to the part.

The next step is to repair or replace any of these parts that are broken or badly worn. If the table's an antique, it's usually a good idea to keep the old pieces even if it means a lot of fixing.

If a mortise is split away or a tenon is broken, they can be repaired the same way as a chair. It is described on page 26. Pieces that are split or broken can be repaired in the same way as a table top.

Before reassembling, clean all dirt, old glue and gunk from every joint. Glue mortise and tenons and reassemble but do not pin. Place the legs on a flat, level surface and clamp across width and along the length. With the clamps tight, drill out old pin holes to make them 1/16" larger and insert new pins of that size, well glued of course. When the glue has cured completely, the joint will be tight.

It is very important that the regluing take place on a flat, level surface because the table will follow the shape of surface it is resting on. Also measure carefully to be sure the aprons are square or at least the same shape they were originally. A good way to tell is to measure from corner to corner before taking the table apart. Then secure the legs and aprons in this shape with diagonal braces while the glue sets. Otherwise, the top will not fit properly.

BROKEN TABLE LEGS AND STRETCHERS

In general, table legs and stretchers can be mended using the same techniques used for chairs. See page 31 for description. There is another type of splint which can be used on the larger legs such as on tables. It is called the spline splint.

Instead of using splints let into mortises on either side of the break, a spline splint is inserted in a slot in the center of the leg. Simply saw a slot about one fourth the thickness of the leg so it runs across the break. An oversize wood spline is inserted, glued and clamped. When the glue cures, cut the excess overlap of the spline away, sand and finish to match the rest of the leg.

The tricky thing about the spline splint is getting the slot cut accurately. Fit the broken ends together accurately and then clamp the leg down so the two pieces are *perfectly lined up*. Use a marking gage and straightedge to scribe the outlines of the cut. Mark both sides accurately since a slight change in the angle of the slot will cause the broken ends to miss alignment. If that does happen with a turned leg, however, trim the jagged ends a little and fill the void area with epoxy putty. If it happens with a square leg, the corners will not line up.

After the slot is cut correctly, cut the spline. Note that this is one of the few cases where the patch is cut last. The spline must be exactly the same thickness as the cut, since an undersize sprine cannot be glued as securely and an oversized spline may split the leg. The width of the spline, however, should exceed that of the table leg at its widest. The excess is trimmed away later.

The same technique can be used for table stretchers. This type break frequently occurs where a cross stretcher is mortised to receive the long stretcher.

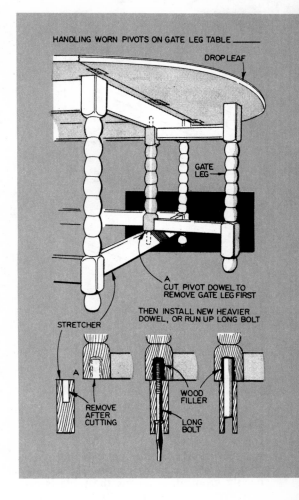

HANDLING WORN PIVOTS ON GATE LEG TABLE

DROP LEAF

GATE LEG

A
CUT PIVOT DOWEL TO
REMOVE GATE LEG FIRST

THEN INSTALL NEW HEAVIER
DOWEL, OR RUN UP LONG BOLT

STRETCHER

A
REMOVE
AFTER
CUTTING

WOOD
FILLER

LONG
BOLT

Mend the broken stretcher first and then make a new mortise.

GATE-LEG TABLES

A popular type of drop leaf table is the gate-leg version with four stationary legs which are more or less conventional, and two extra legs which swing out like a gate to support the hinged leafs. Repair work entails all of the problems found with any other table, plus two others: broken pivots and quarter-circular scars on the underside of the leafs.

The scars on the underside of the leafs are not serious because they do not im-

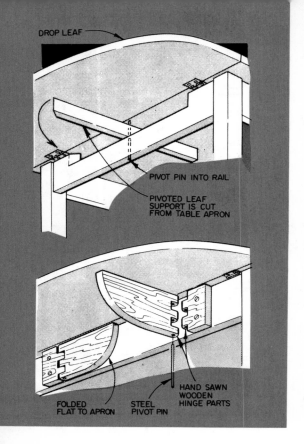

DROP LEAF

PIVOT PIN INTO RAIL

PIVOTED LEAF
SUPPORT IS CUT
FROM TABLE APRON

FOLDED
FLAT TO APRON

STEEL
PIVOT PIN

HAND SAWN
WOODEN
HINGE PARTS

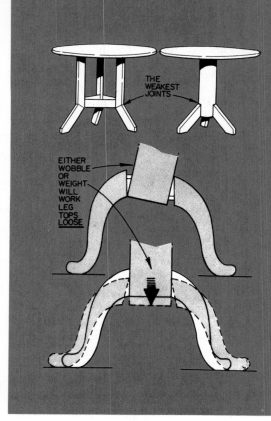

THE
WEAKEST
JOINTS

EITHER
WOBBLE
OR
WEIGHT
WILL
WORK
LEG
TOPS
LOOSE

pair function and they can't be seen except by the nosiest of people. If they are deeply grooved, it means the table is either very old or that the top of the gate leg has some sharp edge which is routing out the wood. If you suspect the latter, remove the leaf and check the leg top. Sand it smooth and work in a little paraffin wax.

The top 'itself may be very soft pine and subject to excess wear. A good soaking in penetrating finish will harden it somewhat. A coat of wax will reduce friction, too.

Occasionally, pivot dowels forming the hinges of the gate leg will break or become loose with wear. If the pivots are metal, it is the holes that are worn, of course. If they are wood dowels, it may be either or both that are worn. The first advice is to try to live with the condition if you can.

If you must repair it, it means replacing the pivot and/or the bushing hole. That is not difficult, but to do a proper job, you must take apart the frame of the table because the pivots are almost always blind. That is, they are installed in the stretcher and rail before the legs are put on and they should be removed in reverse order. That is, legs removed so rail and stretcher can be separated. This need only be done with antiques, however.

The easiest pivot repair method is to cut the lower dowel with a hacksaw blade slipped between the leg and the rail. Then tilt the leg out, lowering it out of the upper pivot hole. Inspect the pivot holes. If they are worn, they can be drilled out to the next larger size providing the rail and stretcher are thick enough. If not, mortise in patches and drill them for the pivots. The hole for the lower pivot must be drilled through the stretcher so the

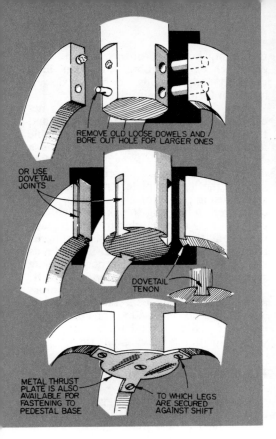

REMOVE OLD LOOSE DOWELS AND BORE OUT HOLE FOR LARGER ONES

OR USE DOVETAIL JOINTS

DOVETAIL TENON

METAL THRUST PLATE IS ALSO AVAILABLE FOR FASTENING TO PEDESTAL BASE

TO WHICH LEGS ARE SECURED AGAINST SHIFT

Joint between leg and stretcher are held by two grooved dowels. Note how stretcher end is concave to receive the round leg. Leg can be mortised flat to receive stretcher.

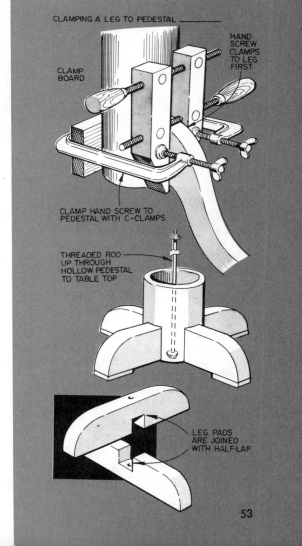

CLAMPING A LEG TO PEDESTAL

HAND SCREW CLAMPS TO LEG FIRST

CLAMP BOARD

CLAMP HAND SCREW TO PEDESTAL WITH C-CLAMPS

THREADED ROD UP THROUGH HOLLOW PEDESTAL TO TABLE TOP

LEG PADS ARE JOINED WITH HALF-LAP

new pivot dowel can be driven in from below. The dowel which was sawed off must be removed or drilled out, of course.

DROP-LEAF PIVOTS AND HINGES

Two other ways of supporting hinged leafs are by a pivoting section of the table rail and by a wooden support hinge.

The pivot support is simple and seldom needs attention. The pivot dowel does not carry any weight, which is balanced between one under the fixed table top and the other end under the hinged leaf. If this type of pivot breaks or the support itself breaks due to mechanical damage, remove the fixed top and replace the support and hinge as required.

Hinged leaf supports are another matter. They are simply wooden hinges with a metal pin and the ills that befall them are many. For those that break, you must take the hinge apart and glue the broken parts back together, if possible. If not, make a new piece or the entire hinge. In fitting the hinge halfs together keep them as snug as possible without binding. Use the broken hinge parts as patterns.

If the metal hinge pin is rusted badly, broken or bent, remove it and install a new pin. A rusted pin will sometimes stick and be very difficult to drive out. Try to drive it out gently with a pin punch, but don't hammer hard or you'll drive the wooden fingers apart too. The best way to remove the pin in many sticky cases is to saw it between every bearing surface with a hacksaw blade. Then drive out each section with a pin punch and the section resting on a solid surface. If the pivot holes are worn, drill out a size larger and install an appropriate hinge pin.

PEDESTAL TABLES

Pedestal tables range from great Victorian monsters to delicate Colonial candel stands but they generally have one problem in common: legs that break where joined to the pedestal.

The reason is obvious. The legs are bent. And are subject to the stresses all bent legs fall heir to. In the drawing, imagine a table with three bent legs. You can see how strong the bend must be to keep the leg from breaking. If you join the upper part of the three legs into one, the pedestal, you still have the same situation. Three weak points where the three legs join the pedestal. And this is the spot where most trouble occurs. The weight of the table forces the lower leg section to thrust outward pulling the joint apart.

The legs are usually joined to the pedestal by dowels or a dovetail slot. Often a metal plate is installed at the base of the pedestal to take up the thrust outward. To disassemble, remove the metal plate and gently knock the leg away from the pedestal. Since it is probably loose or you wouldn't be working on it, you'll be able to see which type of joint connects it to the pedestal. If it's a dowelled joint, knock the legs away at right angles to the pedestal. If it's a dovetail tenon and mor-

tise joint, knock it downward. In both cases, check all around the joint lines carefully for old nails, screws or dowels left from former repair jobs.

With the leg off, make any repairs necessary on them. If it's a tenon joint and the tenon is stripped, make a new double tenon as described on page 28. If it's a dowelled joint, replace worn or broken dowels going to a size larger if necessary.

With the leg completely repaired, reinstall it using plenty of glue. Clamp, using contoured clamping blocks. When the glue has set, remove clamps and replace the metal thrust plate. If there is none, it's a good idea to make one. It can be as simple as a galvanized iron mending plate such as found in any hardware store. Or, for a more professional job, use a brass plate cut to fit the pedestal bottom and legs. It should be insetted, of course, for looks. If you can't find brass, any metal will do, including heavy gauge tin.

FOUR-LEGGED PEDESTAL TABLES

Although many four-legged pedestal tables are constructed just like the three-legged variety, there may be significan differences. They are often made like trestle tables . . . that is the two "H" shaped frames with a common crosspiece which is the pedestal. The legs are really just feet and they are usually crossed one over the other by mortising out half of each as shown in the drawing. There is a center bolt which goes through the top trestle. This arrangement is found in many of the heavy Victorian round dining tables. When this type table becomes loose and wobbly, it is usually because the through-bolt is loose or the mortises where the legs cross have become worn.

To make repairs, turn the table over, remove the top by turning out the screws in the upper trestles and remove the through bolt. The hollow pedestal will usually lift off at that point. If not, it's probably held by nails that someone drove in to try to tighten it once before. Remove them. Then examine the crossover mortises. If they are loose, tighten them with shims, glued and driven in snugly. When the glue is cured, reassemble, tightening the through bolt well.

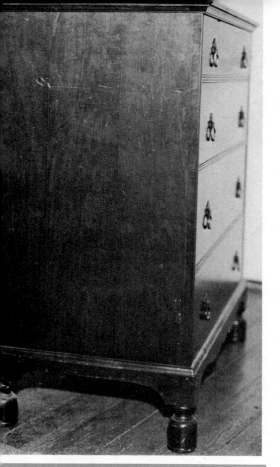

REPAIRING DESKS AND BUREAUS

Cased furniture presents special

problems of repair including

drawers and wide panels.

Solid sides instead of thin panels are typical of this style bureau. This side is in basically good shape despite split off veneer at back edge. These were easily patched to restore.

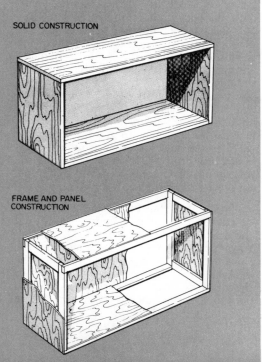

SOLID CONSTRUCTION

FRAME AND PANEL CONSTRUCTION

A ny piece of furniture that has a box-like carcase is called "cased" construction. They include chests of drawers, chests, desks, bureaus, sideboards, cabinets, etc. But for reptair purposes, they can all be lumped together. Fixing a drawer of a desk is just like fixing a drawer of a dresser.

The cases are made one of two ways: solid sides and framed-and-panel sides.

Solid wood construction is literally a variation on the ancient six-board box construction. Frequently, the solid wood is reinforced at corners with glue blocks or braces but this doesn't change their basic nature.

Frame-and-panel construction is used for many reasons. The piece is lighter, less expensive on materials, often more elegant in design and permits the use of several types of wood.

Solid construction has a common fault with sides and top: they can split. Repairing these splits is the same as repairing chair or table splits. The piece should be taken apart as much as possible, and the split cleaned, glued and clamped as de-

This old dresser is structurally sound although painted finish is in terrible shape. Drawer slides and stops had to be repaired to make it completely serviceable again.

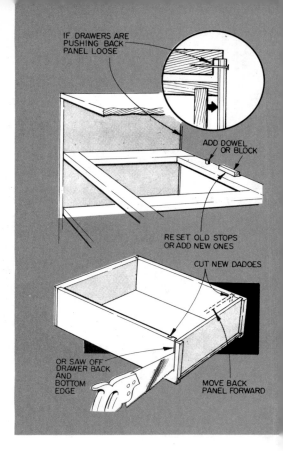

IF DRAWERS ARE PUSHING BACK PANEL LOOSE

ADD DOWEL OR BLOCK

RESET OLD STOPS OR ADD NEW ONES

CUT NEW DADOES

OR SAW OFF DRAWER BACK AND BOTTOM EDGE

MOVE BACK PANEL FORWARD

scribed on page 39. If the wood is sprung and looks as if it may come apart again, make a butterfly patch on the inside to hold it. See page 36.

HOW TO TAKE APART A DRESSER OR DESK

Before attempting to repair any piece of cased furniture such as a desk, bureau or sideboard, take apart everything that can be easily removed. Such as doors and drawers. If the top needs work, remove it too. Such tops are usually fastened from below with screws and/or glue blocks. Others are fastened with dowels. Examine the top carefully, remove all screws and then gently tap from below with soft-faced hammer or mallet. Sometimes it is convenient to remove the top to get at the inside more conveniently for working.

Next, examine the back. It is usually a thin board that is nailed in rabbets in the frame. If it is split, warped or loose, pull the nails with nippers and remove it. Repair the back as much as possible and replace it after all other work on the piece is finished. If the piece is not a valuable antique and the back is badly split, you should replace it with a new back of $\frac{1}{8}''$ plywood, or thicker if the rabbets will take it. The reason is that the back helps hold the piece square and any looseness that causes the piece to get out of square will beget a host of other troubles, such as sticking drawers. In repairing antiques, you should always replace everything you removed from the piece, of course.

One reason that backs of old or cheap cased furniture may come loose is that the drawers hit it when closed. It isn't always poor design but the fact that the sides of the piece shrink, bringing the back closer to the front. But the length of the drawers does not shrink since wood does not shrink along the grain. There

Dust panels separate drawers in the better-built bureaus. If water gets onto panels they are likely to warp badly preventing drawers from sliding properly. Remove or replace.

Bureau drawer slide is badly worn and catches on drawer runner. Simplest cure is a slide button which is nailed at wear spot. Rollers or polyethylene guides could be used.

are usually drawer stops at the back of the rails, either glue blocks or dowels. Make sure the glue blocks are well glued and that dowel stops are not broken. If there are no stops at all, install them at the end of each rail to prevent the drawers from hitting the back of the case, if there is room.

If there is no room to install a stop, the solution is to shorten the drawer or fir out the back. The latter is easiest, since you need only fill in the rabbet with thin strips of wood, glued in place. If the drawer construction is not too complicated, it is best to shorten them to give at least ½″ clearance from the back. Dovetailed drawer ends are very difficult to replace, however. But ends that are held in rabbets are much easier to shorten. Carefully knock drawer apart, saw ½″ off the back end of the drawer sides and recut them to receive the drawer end as before.

DRAWER RUNNERS AND RAILS

The bottom edge of a drawer side is the runner. The board it rides on is the rail. And where they touch, there is constant wear as the drawer is opened and closed. Sometimes the wear is so much that the drawer is loose and will not slide in squarely. Also, it may catch. There are plenty of good solutions to this problem.

First, you can replace the drawer runner. Simply plane down the runner-edge

of the drawer sides and glue on new wooden runners. They should be pine or poplar with the grain running as nearly parallel to the rail as possible. Sand it smooth and wax.

The rail can be replaced, too, but this is a difficult job and not really necessary unless you are a perfectionist. If so, rabbet out the rail until the wear-spots no longer show. Then insert a rail strip, glue, plane smooth and sand. The drawer runner and rail will be good as new.

If you don't want to go to that much trouble, there are easier ways. One is to simply plane the runner as smooth as possible and install plastic "Slide Glides" which are self-lubricating. Simply tack one into each corner where the rail, slide and cross rail meet. The runners ride smoothly on the plastic.

Another way to accomplish the same thing is with a device called a stem bumper. It's really a plastic button with a stem which is pushed into a drilled hole. The face of the button takes the wear, either from draw runner or rail, depending where it's installed.

Another simple way to ease the drawer friction a bit is with nylon tape, made for the purpose and called "Nyl-O-Tape". It is 3/8″ wide and comes in six-foot and larger coils. Remove the paper backing and it will stick tightly to rail or runner and provide a smooth, self-lubricating bearing surface.

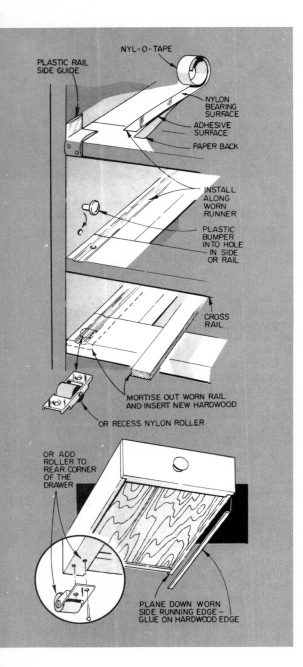

PLASTIC RAIL
SIDE GUIDE

NYL-O-TAPE

NYLON
BEARING
SURFACE

ADHESIVE
SURFACE

PAPER BACK

INSTALL
ALONG
WORN
RUNNER

PLASTIC
BUMPER
INTO HOLE
IN SIDE
OR RAIL

CROSS
RAIL

MORTISE OUT WORN RAIL
AND INSERT NEW HARDWOOD

OR RECESS NYLON ROLLER

OR ADD
ROLLER TO
REAR CORNER
OF THE
DRAWER

PLANE DOWN WORN
SIDE RUNNING EDGE –
GLUE ON HARDWOOD EDGE

Dust panels of a well made bureau. These stop dirt and dust from migrating from one drawer to the next. Sometimes, these panels warp and keep the drawers from sliding.

Yet another commercial solution is to use rollers made especially for drawers. There are several roller systems such as *Roll-eez*, but they do not work for many types of drawers, particularly better bureaus with wide rails. Where there is only a cross rail and a center rail, however, rollers greatly improve drawer function. There are several types, some of which can be recessed into either runner or rail.

DUST PANELS

In better cased furniture there is a thin board between drawers to help keep dust out. It is usually of the same material as the back and frequently installed in slots in the rails. Dust panels don't often need attention but once in a while one will warp so badly that it interferes with the drawers. In such cases, it will be necessary to remove them for repair or replacement. If the panel is in a slot, it is not possible to remove it without taking off the back and perhaps a cross rail at the back. This latter operation is almost impossible without ruining the entire assembly. A somewhat easier method is to cut off the top side of the slot, converting it to a rabbet. Then just lift out the wooden panel. The new panel (or repaired old one) can be glued in place and the slot piece glued over it.

TOPS FOR ROLL-TOP DESKS

There is a great demand for turn-of-the-century roll top desks but few people seem to know how to repair the tops. Repairing the rest presents no unusual problems, but roll tops (known technically as "tambours") seem to confuse people. It is not difficult.

Roll-top desk tambour rides in curved slots in two side pieces. Top can be lifted off, then tambour slides out to repair or replace canvas backing.

Roll top desk tambour rides in curved slots in two side pieces. The top can be lifted off and the tambour will slide out so that the canvas backing can be replaced or repaired as needed.

First, remove the entire top assembly of the desk. This is the unit which contains the tambour, all those little drawers and cubby holes and the grooves that the tambour slides in. To remove it, turn out the four to six screws from underneath the desk top. There may be special hardware holding the top assembly but you'll see it. Remove it and the top will lift off, straight up. It's heavy, though, and it's usually a two-man job.

Place the top assembly on its back so the tambour grooves point approximately up in the air. Pull out the tambour. All the way out. If the slats of the tambour have ripped loose, fish them out of the grooves, too. They may be lying at the bottom of the slot in the back of the desk itself. Place them in order, canvas side up.

Since the fabric backing for the wooden slats is probably old and has lost is strength, replace it completely. Use heavy linen or heavy linen canvas such as used by artists. But before removing the old or replacing it with new, you must have some kind of simple frame to hold the slats while you work.

A sheet of ½" or larger plywood is easiest. It won't be damaged by such use. Lay the slats out on the plywood in order with the canvas side up. Cut a batten to run across the ends of the slats. It should be 1/32" thicker than the slats themselves. Then place another batten over the first one to form a lip. The ends of the slats should rest under this lip. Clamp, nail or screw these two battens in place, holding the slat ends loosely. Repeat for the other end of the slats. Before fastening the second batten and lip, make

59

Lift off the roll top assembly of a roll top desk by removing screw fasteners from below, if there are any, and pry up. Use padding to protect finish from further marring.

sure the slats are perpendicular to the slat. In other words, the two battens are perfectly parallel and the slats are perfectly perpendicular to them. If not, the reglued tambour may not ride easily in the desk slots.

Next, fasten boards to the plywood frame at the ends of the tambour, parallel to the slats. Leave an inch clearance for wedges which will be used to hold the slats together while gluing on the fabric backing.

Remove all the old canvas, using pliers, putty knife and anything else that you think will help. Sand off the old glue to bare wood. At this point you have a bunch of slats with the ends held between long battens and the plywood base.

Apply a flexible glue such as hide glue or Elmer's white glue liberally with a brush. Smooth on the canvas with your hand. The canvas should be at least an inch narrower than the slats, leaving ½"

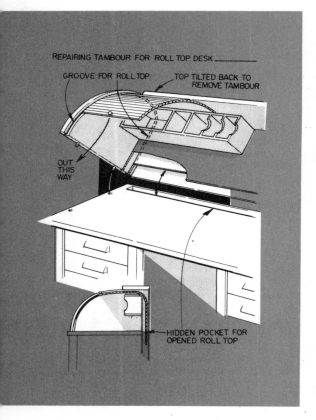

REPAIRING TAMBOUR FOR ROLL TOP DESK

GROOVE FOR ROLL TOP

TOP TILTED BACK TO REMOVE TAMBOUR

OUT THIS WAY

HIDDEN POCKET FOR OPENED ROLL TOP

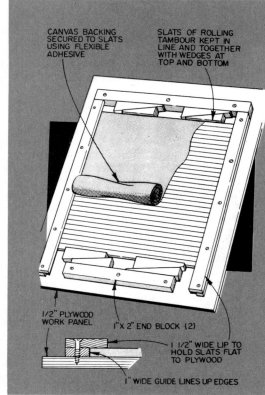

CANVAS BACKING SECURED TO SLATS USING FLEXIBLE ADHESIVE

SLATS OF ROLLING TAMBOUR KEPT IN LINE AND TOGETHER WITH WEDGES AT TOP AND BOTTOM

1/2" PLYWOOD WORK PANEL

1"X 2" END BLOCK (2)

1 1/2" WIDE LIP TO HOLD SLATS FLAT TO PLYWOOD

1" WIDE GUIDE LINES UP EDGES

on either side to ride in the grooves. When the glue is completely cured, remove the gluing frame and reassemble the desk. Rub the ends of the slats and the groove itself with paraffin or candle wax so it will run easier.

HARDWARE AND KNOBS

Hardware such as hinges, catches, locks, escutcheons, fall stays, casters, knobs and handles should be checked carefully. Loose screws must be tightened, but take care not to strip the threads in the wood. If they are already stripped they can be tightened as described on page 56. Or try one of the new wood expanding chemicals such as Chair-Loc, sold at most hardware stores for tightening leg members of chairs.

If knobs or handles are missing, try to replace them at decorator hardware outlets or, if the piece is old, at junk shops. But failing to find a suitable match, it is usually best to replace all the knobs or handles with a matching set.

SIDE PANELS

Many pieces of cased furniture have side panels instead of solid wood or veneer. In time, the panels shrink and become loose in the grooves. If the panels were glued or nailed tightly splits may develop where the ends pull away from each other. In bad cases, you may have to knock the frame apart, remove the panel and reglue it. Most times, however, you can work glue into the split and wedge the pieces together from the back. If that fails, fill the split with plastic wood, stick shellac or water putty since it is not a structural member.

THE EVILS OF HEAT

Most people know the damage done to furniture by excess dampness. Nevertheless, probably most of the troubles that befall wooden furniture are caused by heat. The dry heat found in American houses. Actually, it is not the temperature rise that causes the troubles—it's the lack of humidity. The average American home with hot air furnace has drier air in win-

Drawer construction showing blind dovetail joints at both ends. These are easy to knock apart to repair bottom panel or other pieces, yet they can be re-glued for sturdy joints.

ter than the Sahara desert does at it's worst.

For human beings, it is bad, but they are not the subject of this book. For furniture, it's terrible! It's like having the wood live in an eternal kiln. Wood shrinks and warps. Glue flakes and crumbles. Veneer comes off. Joints don't hold tight.

The answer is, of course, humidity. They can be installed on hot air furnaces but the cost of a good one is rather high. The usual plate type humidifiers are not sufficient to raise the relative humidity to the 30% or more recommended. Unit humidifiers work well in a limited area. The cost of humidifier is somewhat compensated for by the fact that moist air makes you feel warmer than dry air. In a house with sufficient humidity a constant temperature of about 68° will feel like 70° or more. So you save on heating bills.

Excess moisture is also bad as anyone knows who has tried to store good furniture in a damp basement or garage. The humidity affects many types of glue, especially older glues such as hide glue. However, the dangers from excess moisture is less because people recognize it instinctively.

RESTYLING AND RE-UPHOLSTERING OLD FURNITURE

Improve looks and function of furniture by changes in structure, trim, upholstery.

Many pieces of furniture are not used or even discarded because they are ugly or they do not serve some particular purpose. Yet they are structurally sound and sometimes even basically beautiful. The trick is to find ways to improve old furniture by restyling. And on a more obvious level, to improve it by fixing up the worn and torn upholstery. Here are the basics of both. The skilled craftsman will immediately be able to apply these basics to his particular project.

CHANGING STRUCTURAL PIECES

The most common structural change, perhaps, is table legs. Since table tops and legs come apart easily, they can be recombined in almost infinite variety. For legs attached with hanger bolts, you only need to make sure the bolt lines up with the corner brace hole. If it doesn't, rotate the leg 90° and insert the hanger bolt correctly. Often the style of a table can be changed drastically just by changing the legs. New legs of excellent quality can be purchased from most mail order woodworker supply companies.

Old Victorian oak pedestal tables are admired by many but they are too large for the average dining room today. They can be made into beautiful coffee tables, by either removing the top, cutting the pedestal down to 12" or so and re-installing the top. Or simply store the pedestal somewhere and add new screw-on legs.

Structural changes in chairs are not often successful because each one is designed as a unit and by removing the back or a rung, for example, you would weaken the chair so it could no longer be used.

Round Victorian dining tables like this are frequently made into coffee tables for living rooms. Pedestal can be cut down or simply removed and short legs added as desired.

TRIM AND GINGERBREAD

This is the most-often change that people make. It's mostly done to make styles conform. If the rest of your furniture is Early American, for example, you can usually make Victorian pieces match by stripping away the molding on doors, side panels, table aprons and so on. Also by removing the filigree or cutting it down to much simpler lines. Many pieces are covered with cheap veneer which is often in bad shape anyway. The wood underneath can be sanded and stained to achieve an Early American look.

Complicated tables like this gate leg reproduction are not easy to restyle because structure will not hold together. Round solid walnut top, however, could readily be re-used.

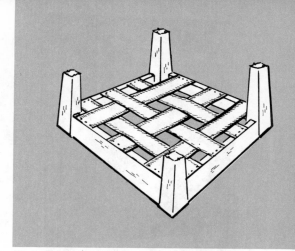

Chair webbing is woven and tacked to frame. Springs in upholstery rest on the intersections where they are tied and sewed in place. Area is finally covered with cloth.

DOORS OR NO DOORS?

Cupboards, sideboards and the like are made more or less formal by adding or subtracting doors. Sometimes the change in style is accomplished beautifully just by the simple expedient of taking the doors off. Or by getting new doors and hanging them on the piece. Simple country styling often suggests removing doors from a cupboard to match the rest of a room. Or, going the other way, glass doors could be added, replacing solid doors or none at all. When old doors are removed, hinge mortices should be patched.

VENEER, GOOD AND BAD

When it comes to restyling, veneer works both ways. Take off old oak or mahogany veneer, sand down the base wood and stain and it will look positively provincial—sometimes. Do not remove old veneer from antiques, however, until you're sure you aren't destroying a great deal of its value. It may be wiser to sell the piece, if you don't like its looks, and buy one you like better. And pocket the difference.

Likewise, a plain, uninteresting piece of furniture can be given new zest for life by adding veneer. Or the new plastic "veneers" such as Micarta or Formica. Veneering can be purchased by mail from

several large woodworker supply companies, complete with simple instructions.

UPHOLSTERY REPAIRS

For some reason, many men shy away from working on upholstered furniture. They are actually quite easy to fix up when you understand the basics, namely a wood frame with metal springs (usually coil) between the members, held in place by wire and webbing below and cord and fabric above. They are then padded and covered with the final fabric.

REPAIRING WEBB BOTTOM SEATS

Tools you will need are tack hammer, ripping tool (tack puller), and curved needles. Materials most needed are tacks, a roll of 3" to 4" webbing, a roll of cotton felt or other stuffing, heavy cord, burlap and a webbing stretcher.

REPAIRING WEBBING ON SEATS

Remove the fabric over the bottom of the seat with a ripping tool. Examine the webbing which is woven across the frame and tacked to it. If it is worn or torn, remove and replace it. First, tie the springs together in place by attaching cord to frame and knotting it to each spring in line across and then tying the cord to the

Old kitchen cupboard was hand made from native walnut and painted. Doors had perforated tin which was replacd with glass for better function and more formal appearance.

opposite frame, pulling it as tight as possible. Do this in two directions. Then tack webbing to one side of the frame and stretch it across the spring bottoms, following the cords. Pull tight with webbing stretcher and tack to opposite frame. Then do the same with webbing at right angles to it, weaving it across. Pull tight and tack.

SEAT PADDING

Carefully untack the top fabric and the under fabric, if any, to expose the old padding. Usually it will be thin, not resilient and probably have slipped away somewhere. Remove it. Re-tie any of the springs that need it, just as for the bottom. Then place burlap over the springs and the padding material over it and tack in place. For arms and some backs, the padding can be placed directly on the wood. Then, in either case, cover the padding with more burlap and tack to the frame also. Use a curved needle and thread to stitch around loosely through the fabric layers and the padding to help hold it in place. Ideally speaking, padding should be in two or three layers, first a layer for springiness, a second layer that combines springiness and smoothness and the third layer which is smooth. The basic springy stuffing is animal hair or its synthetic equivalent, Saran. Others are fibers from moss, palm, coco and one known as Tampico because it comes from a Mexican desert plant. Top layer is usually cotton. When foamed plastic is used, there are no layers of course.

This old dresser can be rebuilt in several ways such as cutting legs off shorter or cutting down frame to eliminate two top drawers. Restyling might include hardware.

Re-upholstering a chair seat takes an understanding of its structure but is not too difficult for the do-it-yourselfer. Here, tacks are driven into frame to hold the spring cords.

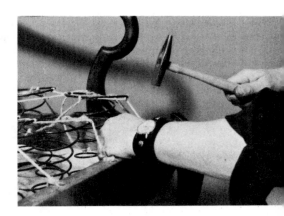

Upholstery springs are held upright by strong cord. Method of lacing and tying is important because it gives them flexibility while holding them in place. Work carefully.

TACKING FABRIC

It's simple but you should develop dead-eye aim with the tack hammer first. Pick up a tack with the magnetic end of the hammer and whack it into a scrap piece of wood, on target. Draw a line and practice driving tacks along the line, one inch apart. Then draw a circle and practice that. Until you never miss.

Spacing of tacks depends on the fabric, of course. Thin silks should be tacked every half-inch. Heavy canvas or leather need be tacked only every 1½ inches.

Blind tacking is commonly used for the finish fabric and is simply turning the edge under, tacking and folding the fabric back over it. This is fine, except for the fourth side. To make the tacks along this edge invisible too, cut a strip of cardboard that conforms to the edge. Push the tacks through it, points toward the wood. Then fold back the fabric with the tack-laden cardboard in place so the points penetrate the fabric, and into the wood. Then tap the tacks in, using several layers of cloth over the hammer to keep the fabric from tearing through.

Upholstered end panels are used to hide the rows of tacks on places like chair arms. Just cut a thin piece of plywood to the shape of the arm end, pad it and cover with fabric, tacking on the reverse side. Use short tacks that won't go through. Then fasten the upholstered panel to the chair arm with a couple of finishing nails, carefully pushed through the fabric and driven home with a nail set.

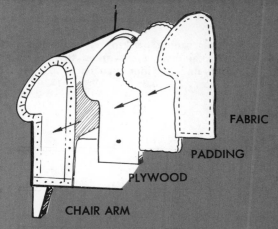

FABRIC

PADDING

PLYWOOD

CHAIR ARM

Blind tacking at end of chair arm is accomplished by using plywood form (Masonite will do) and tacking padding and fabric to it. Headless nails are driven with nail set.

Cross section of chair seat shows how cords are attached to springs and frame to hold them in place. Padding over springs may have fabric under layer, sewed into place.

SINGLE TACK METHOD

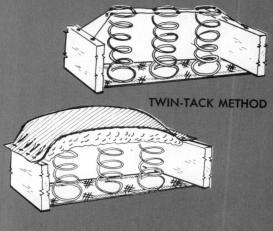

TWIN-TACK METHOD

Knots for tying upholstery cord. After cord is pulled tight the tacks are driven home. Use twin-tack knot when a single cord must carry heavy weight or when wood does not hold.

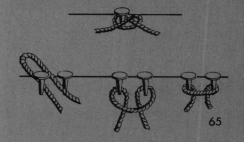

Chair caning patterns vary but this is the most common. Lacing is started in center of vertical rows and worked toward outer edge. This is especially important when front of frame is wider than back, in which case rows are kept parallel with last one or two.

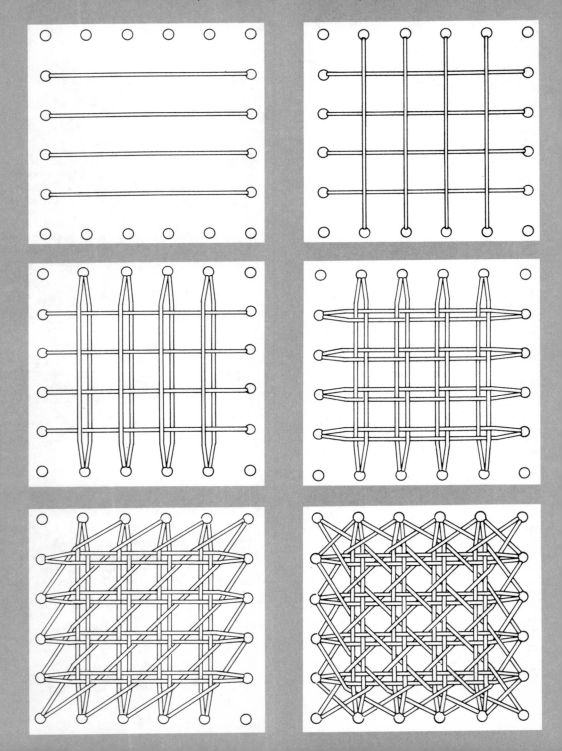

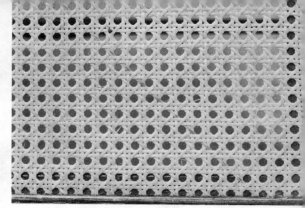

Pre-woven cane can be purchased by the yard and easily installed in seats and backs like this with grooves and splines. It is trimmed to size, soaked to make it supple.

Detail of bench shows where edges of the pre-woven cane have been tapped into the grooves and held in place by wooden splines wedged in. This works very well.

Most tacking will be required to replace the material taken loose in order to add new padding to various parts of the furniture piece. The job of completely recovering a chair or sofa is certainly not impossible for the do-it-yourselfer but because of things like cutting the fabric pattern it is beyond the scope of this book which is concerned primarily with repairs.

SEAT CANING

The most frequent solution to a broken through cane chair seat is usually a piece of plywood, often upholstered. It is not difficult to replace the cane, however. There are two methods, one involving strands of cane which are woven between holes in the chair frame. The other involves pre-woven cane which is held in grooves or slots by a wedged spline driven in flush.

The pre-woven cane can be purchased at many large hardware stores catering to decorators, or from mail order supply houses. To install first remove the old cane. If it has been woven on the chair itself, the pre-woven cane will not work since it must go into the old grooves. Remove the thin wooden splines from the grooves and rout out the old cane there too. It may have been glued, but it has to come clean.

Place the pre-woven cane over the opening and carefully mark the outside edge of the grooves on it, all around. Cut just a hair, say 1/16" outside this line. Then soak the cane in warm water until

soft. While it is soaking, make sure the splines are in good condition. If not, make new ones. Then place the softened cane over the seat so it lines up with the grooves. Coat the splines with white glue and tap one partially in so the edges of the cane are trapped in the groove but not driven tight. Then place the spline in the opposite groove, also trapping the cane ends. Then do the same for the other two sides. When all of the cane ends are trapped in the grooves all around by the splines, they can be driven in. This will pull the cane fairly tight. Take care that there are no wrinkles. Let the cane dry which will shrink it a little tighter. Then plane or sand off the tops of the splines, making them flush. The job's done.

WEAVING CANE

Weaving cane strands on the seat itself is not difficult either, but it does take time and patience. The drawings show how it is done for a perfectly square seat. When the seat is wider at the front, the last couple of front-to-back strands will attach to the side frame holes in order to keep them parallel. The weaving then proceeds as for a square frame. Always start the first strand in the center hole of the front side and go to the center hole of the rear side, working towards both edges. The bitter end is coiled around a strand underneath. The final job can be shellacked, if desired.

The original finish on an old piece of furniture is frequently in excellent shape under layers of dirt. This marble top Victorian bureau was restored beautifully by a really good cleaning.

RESTORING THE OLD FINISH

Look before you strip. The old finish may be beautiful underneath

There are a couple of good reasons to consider saving the old finish. If the piece of furniture is a rare antique, its value will be decreasd by removing it. Also, the finish may be truly beautiful underneath a layer of gunk and grime. Finally, even though the old finish may be crackled, scratched, blotched and chipped, you may find it easier to restore than to strip and refinish.

HOW TO TELL WHAT
FINISH IS ALREADY THERE

There are three common types of finish that you are likely to find on factory-made furniture ... even dating back to pre-Civil War days. One, shellac. Two, lacquer. Three, shellac-varnish mixture. In addition, there is varnish, plus natural wax and oil finishes, all of which are the mark of the restorer and custom cabinet-maker.

Shellac finish—this is the oldest type and was used exclusively on manufactured furniture up through the Civil War. It softens and dissolves in denatured (not rubbing) alcohol, and therein lies the best test. First, remove any wax with turpentine or wax remover. Wet the corner of a soft cloth in denatured alcohol and rub it into the finish. Keep wetting the cloth and wetting for 5 to 10 minutes. If the finish is shellac, it will soften and start to spread again.

Lacquer finish—used on furniture made after World War I because it can be sprayed on and dries in minutes. The solvent for lacquer is made largely of acetone and is sold as "lacquer thinner". Remove any wax first. Then make the same test as above wetting a bit of cloth with it and rubbing into the finish. If it softens, it is certain to be a lacquer finish. Lacquer thinner will also soften some shellac finishes but no kind of denatured alcohol will soften a lacquer finish. So it is important to make the test with alcohol first.

Shellac-lacquer finish—there was a time from the 1850s to about 1920 when after removing all traces of wax, the denatured alcohol test produces some softness but not enough to rework the finish, try the lacquer thinner test. This will soften both ingredients, but the fact that alcohol had some effect probably indicate shellac-lacquer mixed. So mix alcohol and lacquer thinner.

Varnish finish—if none of the above tests faze the finish, it is probably varnish. Or that you forgot to remove the protective wax coating. Varnish was and is rarely used in production work because the time to dry and cure is days instead of minutes. Sometimes it was used by custom cabinetmakers and it is frequently used by refinishers. It's a beautiful finish and very tough and pliable, which makes it particularly attractive for ship masts and spars. It is also fairly impervious to alcohol. Perhaps the easiest way to tell varnish is by the "look". It has a deep, rich, softly luxurious look compared to the crystal-hard look of lacquer or the thin, watery look of most shellac. There is another test, too: crease the finish with your

Badly scratched surfaces like this may not be as bad as they seem. Only one of these marks was deep enough to affect the wood. The old finish had to be removed, however.

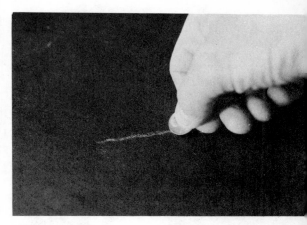

The coin test of an old finish. If you can break down the finish to bare wood with the edge of a coin, it should be refinished. Otherwise finish can probably be restored.

This much-abused dresser looks bad here, but it is structurally sound and has beautiful curly maple veneer which makes it well worth refinishing. All new hardware used.

This handsome piece had many layers of paint and tin instead of glass in the doors. Stripping revealed it to be solid walnut. Beauty of wood justified removing paint.

This interesting spool leg table had a perfectly good finish under years of accumulated dirt and grime. Mild soap and warm water, or a mild detergent removed most.

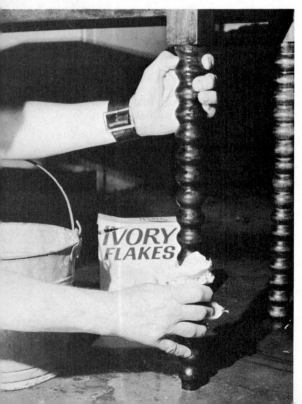

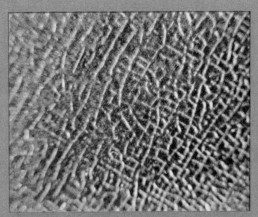

Alligatored finish, shown here larger than actual size, is a frequent problem with old finished. Lacquer and shellac can often be reamalgamated, varnish almost never can.

thumbnail. If it leaves a slight dent where the finish "gives", instead of showing no mark or chipping slightly, it is probably varnish.

Painted finishes—you won't have any problem recognizing it, of course, but there may be some other course between stripping the piece completely and just painting over the paint. Many antique pieces such as American Windsor chairs were painted originally. It may still be there, underneath many subsequent paint layers, ready to be revealed again. Check around the hidden parts of the piece, such as the leg sockets of chairs. Often, you'll see a history of the piece in layers of paint. A little scraping there will help you reveal them. If there is still the original layer of paint, it may be as valuable as the furniture, especially if it has stenciled designs. The trick is to remove the outer layers and leave it. Use hand scrapers and sandpaper only so you'll have enough control to stop short of the original paint. Chemical paint removers may cut through to bare wood so fast you can't stop if the original paint was so-called "milk" paint, it will not be affected by most commercial paint removers, but you're never sure until it's too late.

If the color is in a lacquer base, lacquer thinner will soften it. Then you can

Wax may have built up over many years, trapping dirt under it. It must be removed before you can work on the old finish. Special wax removers like this make it easy.

Paint thinner or turpentine and fine steel wool can be used to remove stains that are on top of the finish. Use steel wool lightly so as not to rub through finish to wood.

re-amalgamate the finish as described below.

In any case, if you do attempt to remove the top layers of paint and preserve the lowest layer, you're in for a big job. The final results will be interesting however, usually an earthy red, green or black paint, probably with lots of scratches and chips. See chapter 12 for repairs, and remember that on some antiques, the original finish may be as valuable as the furniture.

CLEANING UP AN OLD FINISH

Just because the furniture piece looks dark and murky, lacks life and warmth, don't jump to the conclusion that you have to strip it to bare wood and start over. In a great many cases the old finish can be brought to life with a good scrubbing. The results are sometimes better than you could achieve in a weekend of refinishing.

Now that does not imply that you don't keep your furniture clean. Or that previous owners haven't. But grease, oil, dirt, carbon and lots of other things get on furniture over the years, from dirty fingers and smoky fires and who knows what. Most of it was washed off, let's say,

immediately. But some remained and worked its way into the finish. And later layers of wax and polish sealed in it. And in 10 to 20 years, the look of the finish changes, losing its richness and luster.

How you remove the aged-in dirt depends on what kind of finish it is. Varnish can be cleaned up with solutions containing water. Shellac and lacquer finishes cannot, since they absorb water and develop white spots. But in either varnish or shellac-lacquer finishes, the first step in cleaning is to remove all traces of old wax.

GETTING THE WAX OFF

A typical furniture paste wax is compounded of 25 per cent wax and 75 per cent mineral spirits. The type of wax used varies, but a common formula is 10 per cent hard wax such as beeswax or carnauba and 15 per cent pure paraffin. The ingredients are mixed at high temperature and become a paste at room temperature.

All paste wax provides good protection against water, in addition to a glossy shine. But this water-resistance also makes it necessary to remove the wax before you try to clean the furniture.

Lacquer finish on this bureau top has become dull and cloudy due to sunlight and age. Note glossy streaks where finish remained intact. It can be easily restored.

Lacquer thinner brightens the finish by softening it and reflowing it over surface. A fine grade steel wool can spread the process. Work quickly because lacquer dries fast.

Magnified view of a finish that has become badly checkered. Varnish like this can sometimes be improved by a 2-2-1 mixture of varnish, boiled linseed oil and turpentine.

Water soluable dirt may be sealed under the wax, untouched by any number of well-meaning washings.

There are many commercial preparations for removing wax. Lemon oil is one. Most contain a high percentage of mineral spirits, also known as mineral oil.

It is less expensive to use mineral spirits in the first place. It may be warmed a little to make it work faster. The wax becomes soft and wipes right off. Use a soft cloth and give the mineral spirits plenty of time to work. It will also dissolve grease and oil too.

Turpentine will also dissolve wax and can be used in the same way as mineral spirits, including heating. If you use turpentine first, finish with a quick wiping with mineral oil. And in either case, wipe dry with a clean cloth.

After the wax is removed, if the finish looks a lot better, it simply means there was a lot of dirt and stuff imbedded in the wax. If it does not look better (or looks worse because the wax shine is gone), don't worry. It may come alive with subsequent steps.

WASHING A VARNISH FINISH

Actually, you can wash any finish with water, but shellac and lacquer finishes tend to develop a kind of milky whiteness. It is actually the same thing that happens when you leave a water mark with a water glass. It isn't difficult to cure. See page 76.

Varnish, on the other hand, was developed for its water resistance and can be scrubbed with soap and water. The only danger there would be to veneers. The glue could easily soften and cause the veneer to come loose. Use warm water and mild soap like Ivory or Lux flakes. Some people add a couple of tablespoons full each of turpentine and boiled linseed oil to the washing solution, but if you washed down with them first, it is not necessary. The soap and water treatment will help remove all traces of oil and spoons full of sal soda to the wash water will help remove all traces of oil and grease. Carved areas, flutings, cornices and other irregular spots should be scrubbed with a mild brush like a toothbrush. Wipe completely dry after washing. If the finish now looks clean and in good shape, you can simply re-wax it or use furniture polish, making sure the piece is completely dry before you do so.

If the finish still has problems, there are still things you can do that are easier than trying to strip and refinish.

RENEWING A CLOUDY FINISH

The milky, cloudy areas on a finish are caused by water. It may be a ring left by the condensation on a glass or it may be the humidity in the air. But alcohol and lacquer can absorb water. And when it evaporates out, the structure of the finish is changed. There is the film-like whiteness or cloudiness often called "bloom."

The old wives answer is cigar ashes and butter. A modern answer is 4/0 steel wood and mineral oil. Both are correct. The ashes act as a mild abrasive and the butter as a lubricant. Professional refinishers often use rottenstone and mineral spirits or 000 Grade steel wool and mineral oil. By lightly rubbing the mild abrasive over the cloudy area, you actually remove a microscopic layer of the finish, leaving the good finish.

Apply soft ashes, rottenstone or (in extreme cases) 4/0 pumice with a pad of felt or layers of soft cotton rags, attached to a wood block. Mix the abrasive and oil to a cream-like consistancy and gently rub with the grain over the blemished area. On varinish finishes, you can use water with the rottenstone since it won't affect the finish.

If you use 4/0 steel wood and oil, you do not need a separate abrasive, of course. Rub softly with the grain using a small amount of mineral spirits and working small patches, one at a time. Wipe dry with soft cloth before proceeding.

If the finish is full of tiny cracks (called "alligatored") in addition to being cloudy, skip the treatment for the latter and proceed with the treatment for alligatoring. It will automatically cure the cloudiness.

ALLIGATORED FINISH

An old finish that has been in the sun may develop large areas that are full of

White rings and marks on a shellac finish can often be removed the "old-wives" way: with cigar ashes and butter or cooking oil. The ashes are actually a very mild abrasive.

Rub the ashes over the white marks using a soft cloth wrapped around a block. Use circular motion, light pressure. Add ashes as needed. Wipe off when marks disappear.

Badly cracked finish on the arm of a chair is being reamalgamated by brushing on lacquer thinner. This melts lacquer so it can be brushed to its original smoothness.

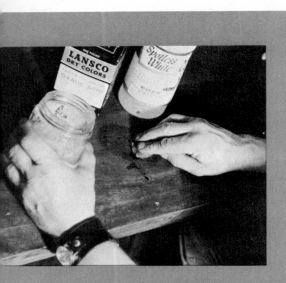

Ink stains on a desk top can often be removed with laundry bleach, ammonia or an oxalic acid. If stain does not penetrate finish, job is easy. Otherwise color may change.

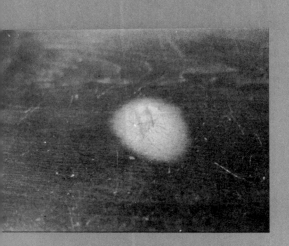

White spots like this on a shellac finish are caused by water. A soft cloth dampened with denatured alcohol can be used to rub the spot out. Or—use oil and rottenstone.

hairline cracks. The tiny cracks are called "crazing," the larger cracks, "alligatoring". They happen when the bright sunlight heats up the dark finish, sometimes as high as 150 degrees. The oils that give the finish its pliability and life are boiled away and the finish separates.

Don't give up on an alligatored finish, no matter how bad it seems. Because if it is lacquer or shellac, you can rework it again and it may come out beautiful. A varnish finish is more difficult to correct because there are few available solvents which will make it melt, once it has cured completely. There are practical ways to improve an alligatored varnish finish, however, if you should encounter one.

Reamalgamation—this is the process of melting the finish with its own solvent. For lacquer, it is lacquer thinner. For shellac, it is denatured alcohol. For some early 20th Century furniture, the best solvent may be a mixture of 3 parts denatured alcohol to one part lacquer thinner.

The technique of reamalgamation is the same for both lacquer and shellac. Only the solvent changes. Apply solvent. Watch carefully until the finish softens. Then smooth or stroke it out with a clean brush or soft cloth. For small areas, a cloth is fine. For larger areas, on an entire piece, use a brush that is absolutely, scrupulously clean.

The first step is to remove all traces of wax with mineral spirits or turpentine, as outlined on page 71. Second, apply the lacquer thinner or denatured alcohol with a brush, working it across the grain just as if you were painting it. Third, when the finish starts to melt, brush it again, this time with the grain. Keep adding solvent as necessary. Both alcohol and lacquer thinner are very volatile and evaporate quickly.

You may leave brush strokes but it is no more serious than when applying a completely new finish. As the finish sets, the strokes tend to fill in somewhat. And minor blemishes can be corrected by a rub down with 3/0 steel wool after the finish dries completely.

If the reamalgamating process becomes streaky from wood stain, it means that the finish is very thin or that the stain was mixed with it when originally applied. There isn't much that can be done about it and if the results are not satisfactory, you will have to add more solvent and wipe away as much as the finish as necessary to produce a nice look. Then apply new lacquer or shellac over it.

CRACKED VARNISH
AND WHAT TO DO ABOUT IT

The reamalgamation process which works so effectively with lacquer and shellac is quite difficult to accomplish with varnish. The solvents for lacquer and shellac will soften them over and over again so they can be reworked many times. But turpentine, the solvent for varnish, will not soften it once it has cured. In fact, there is no common household substance which will soften varnish enough so it can be reworked. There are uncommon chemicals which will work, however. These special "amalgamators" are available at bigger paint and hardware stores under various trade names. They are pretty strong stuff, however, consisting mainly of ether, acetone and other harse chemicals. Supposedly, when spread over the cracked varnish finish, they melt it so it runs together. And when it dried, the surface is smooth again. The success of these "amalgamators" is somewhat limited and it should be tested on an obscure area of the finish before application where it shows.

Another method which sometimes works, depending on how old the varnish is and how deeply cracked, is to fill them with a thin varnish mixture. A good formula consists of 40 per cent varnish, 40 per cent boiled linseed oil and 20 per cent turpentine. Rub into the cracks with a gentle circular motion until it starts to set up. Then wipe away what's left and let what is left in the cracks dry. If necessary, repeat the operation after the first coat is completely dry.

STAINS, RINGS
AND OTHER THINGS

These are the kinds of blemishes that usually occur in some highly visible place and make you think of refinishing the entire piece. They are almost never as serious as they first appear.

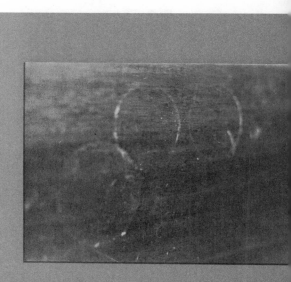

White rings on this shellac finish were caused by the water condensing on cold drinking glasses. Because shellac absorbs water and turns white, waxing is important.

Black rings are caused by water being absorbed into the wood pores. To remove, apply oxalic acid or bleach with artist's brush. If wood lightens, darken with stain.

Grease spots in bare wood will keep any new finish from adhering properly. They can be soaked out with benzine. Apply liberally and wipe dry. Continue until clean.

Cigarette burns can be a serious problem. They must be sanded out and the wood feathered into the finished surface. The entire area must then be stained to match.

Scratches like this are so bad that it is necessary to remove finish entirely. Those that go through into the wood itself must be sanded out before the new finish goes on.

Examine the blemish carefully to determine whether it is on the finish itself, or in the wood beneath the finish. First, things on top of the finish.

Usually surface stains, rings and discolorations are not very deep. They can be eroded away with mineral spirits and a mild abrasive. The general treatment is the same as for a cloudy finish. The difference is that the area of a stain is usually much less, so you can afford to devote a little more time and effort per square inch.

Cigar ashes, pumice, rottenstone, a dishwashing scouring powder such as Ajax or extra fine steel wool will usually take away surface stains and things. Use mineral spirits and work gently, of course. Once the blemish is removed, the finish will probably be somewhat dulled by the scouring. A coat of wax or polish will usually restore the shine enough to match. But you may have to restore a little more finish to the area. In the case of lacquer or shellac, a little of their thinners rubbed in will cover it. For a varnish finish, use new varnish mixed with boiled linseed oil and turpentine and gently rub in.

Some blemishes penetrate the finish, of course, and get into the wood. In such cases, the stain remover has to get to the wood the same way the stain did—namely through the finish. Which means refinishing that area later.

White spots and rings that are in the wood can be removed by adding some of the solvent of the finish to the surface, assuming it is lacquer or shellac. Wet a small pad with the solvent and gently wipe it over the stained area. Keep at it until the stain disappears. When the area dries, it may be much glossier than the rest of the finish. If so, it can be dulled with extra fine steel wood. Then wax the entire surface.

Black spots which have gotten into the wood are usually caused by water discoloration. They can be bleached out easily with oxalic acid crystals dissolved in water. The trick is to apply it sparingly, especially to woods that have been stained, so the black is removed and no serious amount of stain. If so, you may have to remove the finish from all of the surrounding area and treat it evenly with the oxalic acid solution. Then restain, if necessary, and refinish that area. Wash away the oxalic acid solution with vinegar and water before any refinishing.

Ammonia is often useful in removing black stains, ink and other discolorations which have penetrated the wood. Apply to actual stain with small brush. Here again, its action may bleach the wood too much in the stain area and require a much broader area to be treated to match.

Grease spots which have penetrated to the wood can be removed with common household "dry cleaners" such as Energine, in the case of animal fats. Or with benzine. Vegetable oils can be removed with acetone. In either case, apply with a small brush to the specific area and blot up with facial tissue. Several applications may be required to remove it all.

BURNS, CUTS AND DEEP GASHES

The first step in repairing and refinishing any defect which has damaged the base wood is to clean out the damaged area thoroughly. A deep cut which has gone for years unmended is likely to be clogged with all kinds of dirt, wax, grease, etc. The best way to remove it is by scraping with a sharp knife, going all the way to bare wood. Then the cut can be filled and finished as described below.

For burns, the problem is slightly different in that usually more surface area and less depth is involved. Scrape away the charred wood to clean bare base wood. If the hole is deep, it must be filled. If not, it can sometimes be feathered into the surrounding surface with sandpaper and refinished to be barely noticeable. How well the repair blends in depends more on the surrounding finish than on anything you can do. A mirror finish on a perfectly flat tabletop certainly will show up even the slightest indentation. But on a curved surface with satin finish, a feathered-in indentation may be imperceptible.

Shallow cuts and scratches can usually be filled with the finishing material itself. Thus, on a shellac finish you can usually get away with simply filling the scratch carefully with more shellac, applying it in

Gouges and holes in an otherwise good finish can be repaired easily with Plastic Wood. Take special care not to spread too much because it is difficult to get up.

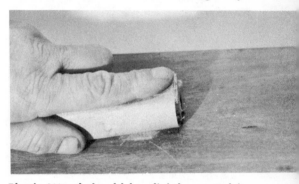

Plastic Wood should be slightly crested in the hole and then sanded down to the surface level after it has thoroughly dried. Use 6/0 sandpaper on a flat block—on area only.

Shellac sticks are used to make more permanent repairs on holes and gouges. Many colors are available to match any finish. Melt and mix sticks to get the right color.

Stick shellac is melted over alcohol lamp. Melted stick shellac is dripped into hole and smoothed down with hot spatula or knife. An alcohol lamp is used because it does not leave soot on blade. Hard patch is sanded.

A spatula for applying stick shellac can be made quickly from old hacksaw blades. Grind off teeth and break to length desired. Then tape between two small wood blocks.

several layers to build it up to surface level. Always use the same finishing material, however. First, stain cut the match finish. Then apply with a sharp stick and be careful to keep it away from the surrounding finish. Wipe up any spills immediately. Let each layer dry completely before going to the next. When layers, with drying time in between. The finish, polish down with pumice and oil or water, depending on type of finish. See page 71.

When a cut, burn or scratch is very deep, it must be filled. There are two basic materials for filling. Stick shellac and plastic wood. Plastic wood comes as a brand-name produce or you can make a suitable filler out of casein glue and sawdust. In every case, select a filler material that matches the finished wood as closely as possible.

When using plastic wood or homemade filler, tamp it in as tightly as possible, making sure not to get any on the surrounding finish. If the hole is very deep, the filling process may require several layers, with drying time inbetween. The depth to which you fill the hole depends on how well the filler matches the surrounding finish. The best way to find out is to test. Put some plastic wood on a scrap board, let dry and sand smooth. Then stain and finish. Experiment until you get an exact match. If you cannot achieve a match because of the surface texture of the filler, use stick shellac for the final layer, over the plastic wood.

Since plastic wood and most fillers shrink, fill slightly above the surface level and sand slugh with 6/0 finishing paper on a hard, flat block and finally going to pumice and mineral spirits. Reamalgamate the finish over the repaired area, if possible. Or refinish to match and polish.

STICK SHELLAC REPAIRS

Stick shellac is also called sealing wax although it is not a wax. But this gives a clue to how you use it. For highly polished finishes, stick shellac can produce almost invisible repairs. Remember, however, that it is opaque and where the repair covers visible wood grain, it will show.

Using stick shellac sounds a little simpler than it is. Just melt the wax, spread it into the hole or crack, shave it off flush, sand and finish.

Stick shellac is available in dozens of standard colors. It is available at larger paint supply stores or the mail-order woodworker supply houses such as Constantine's.

Select shellac of the color that most nearly matches the finish and complete the match at the last stage, if necessary, with stain in the finishing material. The sticks can be blended in a molten state for in-between colors.

There is a little trick to applying stick shellac, in that if you try to melt it with a tool that is too hot it may burn, bubble or discolor. A multi-heat soldering iron is ideal, but a spatula, knife or screwdriver heated over an open flame will do the job nicely. Professionals allegedly use alcohol lamps to heat their tools because the flame does not deposit carbon on the blades. Carbon will discolor the shellac, of course. However, it is a simple matter to heat the tool, quickly wipe the blade, and apply it to the shellac stick with enough heat left to melt it.

Technique of using stick shellac is simple. Heat the tool, melt a small portion of the shellac and drip it or spread it into the hole or crack. Since it may harden, you will have to reheat the tool several times. When the hole is filled above surface level, shave it down with a single-edge razor blade or a sharp chisel. Then sand flush with 6/0 sandpaper on a small flat sanding block. Then refinish and polish to blend in with surrounding finish. If the shellac color is slightly off color after sanding, add a little stain to perfect the match before refinishing.

PATCHING WITH WAX

Cracks, scars and holes can be patched with special wax sticks in almost the same manner as with shellac sticks. Except wax is a lot easier to use, and not nearly as permanent. In fact, where there is a lot of wear, wax patching will probably not be suitable.

Special wax sticks are made for the purpose and come in sets of assorted col-

Stick wax, also called furniture putty, can be used for quick repairs. Sticks come in all furniture colors and can be heated and mixed. Scrape off excess, let dry and shellac.

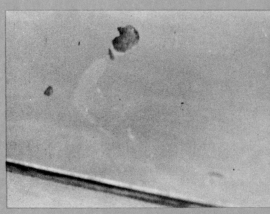

Painted finishes often chip like this, due to some external blow or poor adhesion of the paint. It can be filled with white glue and painted, or feathered down with sandpaper.

Paint chip hole is feathered down with sandpaper. Use 4/0 grade to make work go faster since the paint will flow over and make it smooth again. Wipe away dust beforehand.

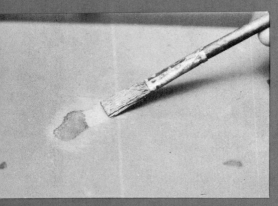

Feather chip hole is painted to match rest of the finish. Use same paint if available. Otherwise mix to match. Use same type of paint so surfaces will look alike, and sand.

Most refinishers have a favorite way to do French Polishing. For restoring an old finish, make polishing ball of soft cloth and soak in thin shellac, then a few drops of linseed oil.

ors. You can also use crayons, melting and blending them together to get just the right color to match your finish. Another technique is to use paraffin or bees wax, or a combination, adding analine dyes or artists dry colors to achieve the right color match.

Wax should be applied just like stick shellac. The scar or hole must be thoroughly cleaned first. Then, if the wax color matches, simply drip the wax into the scar using a source of heat that won't smudge. A soldering iron works well, as does an alcohol lamp or a well adjusted gas burner. If the wax must be blended for color, melt it in a small container and blend. Then you'll have to let it harden to check the color. Then melt and apply as above.

When the wax in the scar has hardened slightly, scrape it off neatly with a single edge razor blade. Let it harden completely and seal it with a light coat of shellac. Varnish or lacquer will react with the wax and not harden properly. Once the shellac has set, you can apply varnish or lacquer to match the rest of the finish.

PEELING AND CHIPPING PAINT

Chipping is caused by some external blow to the finish and is usually confined to a small area. Peeling is caused by some lack of adhesion between finish and the wood. It is usually due to faulty application such as dirt, grease or oil on the wood, too much moisture or inferior paint.

First, test to see whether the finish is an enamel paint or varnish or a colored lacquer. To test, apply lacquer thinner. If nothing happens, it's enamel paint. If the finish softens, it's lacquer. Prospects for an invisible mending job are not good in either case, but since the possible cures are fairly easy, they are worth trying before you strip and start over.

Chipped lacquer finishes are easier. Soften the area around the chipped spot and reamalgamate the finish over it. If the chip is too large for reamalgamation, feather the edges with thinner and apply matching lacquer in the thin layers to cover the spot.

Chipped enamel is handled in similar fashion, except that it cannot be softened with solvent. Feather the edges of the chipped spot with sandpaper and apply the same or matching enamel to the spot, also in thin layers. Give each layer of enamel at least 24 hours to dry before adding another layer. Then use 6/0 abrasive paper and a hard flat block to sand flush.

For a polished finish on either enamel or lacquer, use 4/0 pumice and then rottenstone with mineral spirits to polish. For a satin finish, use extra fine steel wool.

Peeling paint is more difficult to handle and probably can't be cured. But if the peels are still flexible and smooth, you can sometimes rebond them to the wood just as you would loose veneer. Work white glue such as Elmer's under the peeled area and clamp the surface down. Use wax paper and wipe away excess glue carefully. If the cause of the peeling was moisture in the wood which has since dried out, the glue may hold. If not, you aren't out much time or money. Go ahead and strip the piece and start over.

FRENCH POLISHING
TO REVIVE A FINISH

A version of the classic French polishing technique is a wonderful way to revive a dreary finish. Or to repair the finish over an area that has been patched and cannot, for some reason, be reamalgamated. French polishing, in the classic furniture, was a technique for hand-rubbing on multiple layers of shellac to produce a tough finish with a very high sheen. It is the kind of high-gloss finish that is not as stylish today as it was in the days of Louis 14th.

Basically, shellac is applied with an oiled cloth pad, using a non-stop circular or figure-eight motion. The pad can be made from old cloth that is clean and soft. The outer layer must be absolutely lint-free. Make a cloth ball about the size of a baseball, wrapped and tied in the outer cloth.

The first step is to clean the old finish thoroughly with mineral spirits or turpentine and wipe clean and dry. Then dip the polishing pad in shellac that is water thin. This is about a 1-pound cut, or ordinary store shellac that is diluted 50% with alcohol. Squeeze the pad until it is moist but

Technique of French Polishing requires a circular motion that never stops on the wood surface. Slide pad off wood to add a teaspoon of shellac and a few drops of oil.

not dripping. Then place a few drops of raw linseed oil on the pad and start polishing.

It is important never to stop the motion of the pad on the finished surface, once you've started. Develop a rotary motion and slide the pad onto the surface while making the motion. Slide it off the same way. Apply a moderate amount of pressure to force the shellac and oil into the minute grain and other crevices and rub until no more shellac is being deposited. Slide the pad off, add a teaspoonfull of shellac and a few more drops of oil and slide it back onto the finished surface. Continue this procedure until the entire surface is covered and has a shiny look. At this point, do not add more shellac or oil to the pad but keep rubbing until the surface is dry. Then let it set for 24 hours. After that, you can apply another coat if you think it necessary for looks or toughness. Any oil that remains on the surface should be wiped away with a clean cloth soaked in turpentine and wrung dry. Then wipe with a creal, dry cloth.

Although French polishing is not difficult, it does require a little practice. Do not practice on a fine piece of furniture that you are restoring. Try it once or twice on something less cherished until you get the hang of it. There is another nice thing about French polishing: if you make a mistake, such as stopping the pad and leaving cloth marks, you can simply wash the whole thing off with denatured alcohol and start over.

This 60-year-old kitchen cabinet was originally covered with white lacquer. Now, with careful stripping to reveal the handsome wood grain, it has been promoted to sideboard duty.

STRIPPING THE OLD FINISH

It's not as difficult as people think . . . when you know how

When there is nothing you can do to restore the old finish, then you have to remove it. It just isn't possible to put a good finish on top of a bad one.

Fortunately, stripping off paint and varnish is a lot easier than it was even a few years ago. The difference is chemistry . . . greatly improved commercial paint removers now available to the public. De-

spite improvements, however, stripping is still a messy job and it still requires a bit of manual labor.

It is unfortunate that some manufacturers have oversold their "miracle" paint removers to the point where people are disappointed because they expect it to be easier than it really is. Yet by any standard, removing paint and varnish is fairly

This old chair is one of a set and therefore deserves restoration. Finish must be stripped off completely and old leather seat cushions replaced, probably with a durable plastic.

Dark heavy oak bench can be made much happier with a good refinishing job. The old finish and stain come off easily, revealing light grain. Covered pad added color.

easy to do—messy, of course, but also easy. You can strip any piece of furniture in one Saturday afternoon without working up a sweat.

CHEMICAL PAINT REMOVERS

There are many grades of chemical paint and varnish removers on the market and generally you get what you pay for. So price is usually a good indication of quality, especially if the manufacturer has a complete line of stripping agents. Look for one that is water washable or one that does not require a neutralizing agent for cleaning up afterward. Look for one that is nonflammable. And look for one that does not produce dangerous fumes. All these things should be stated on the label. While these characteristics in a paint remover are valuable in themselves as convenience and safety factors, they also indicate product quality which includes other characteristics such as faster working time and easier application.

Paint removers generally contain wax-like chemicals to prevent solvents from evaporating. They can be deposited on the bare wood after all the paint is gone. It will prevent the new finish from adhering properly. So you have to wash it off with benzine, turpentine, lacquer thinner or some other solvent. The more expensive paint removers such as Klean-Strip and Strypeez contain emulsifiers so the wax will dissolve in water and wash away during the rinse.

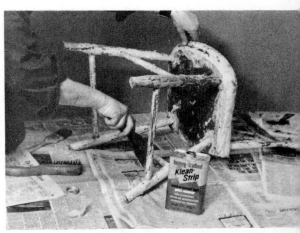

Apply stripper and wait five to 30 minutes until paint blisters and loosens. Use scraper to remove large areas of paint. In warm weather it's preferable to work out of doors.

Stripping materials are few and not expensive. A few rags, scraper, pocket knife, wire brush, coarse steel wool, a good brand of paint remover and an old brush to apply it.

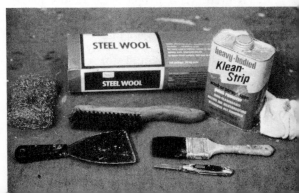

Paint peels off in sheets from top of a large painted table, turned on its side to get rid of peelings easier. The surface was then scoured with wire brush and lots of water.

Frame of this old mirror was stripped to show off beauty of the natural birds-eye maple frame. Here, hose and a wire brush get off most paint. Use steel wool to finish.

Stripping small pieces like this chair are done indoors quite easily. After getting off bulk of paint with scraper, coarse steel wool is used. Many people wear rubber gloves.

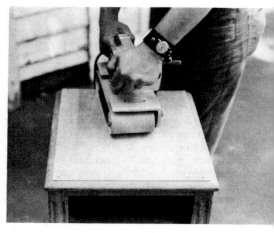

Electric sanding is not usually recommended for stripping because it's expensive for the sanding belts and not as fast as chemicals. Epoxy enamel on this bedtable needed it.

Paint removers generally come in two consistencies: liquid for ordinary work when the surface can be held flat and paste for vertical surfaces.

The first step in stripping is to find a place to do it. If the weather is reasonably warm, do it out of doors. Otherwise,

the garage or basement will suffice, provided you can splash around plenty of water. Wear old clothes and old shoes or rubber boots and rubber gloves if your hands are sensitive to strong chemicals.

When using some types of paint removers, you may not have to take such precautions, but check the label carefully. Also note whether full ventilation is required.

You won't need much equipment. An old brush or two, a few empty coffee cans, a flexible putty knife with the sharp corners rounded off, a medium wire brush, some coarse steel wool, some old rags and perhaps a toothbrush for getting into carvings and crevices.

HOW TO APPLY PAINT REMOVER

There is one thing to remember: put it on thick and leave it alone. The solvents in the formula do two things—they soften the paint and they evaporate into the air. If you stir them around with the brush, they evaporate faster and soften slower. But if you apply the paint remover as thickly as possible and let stand, a wax film forms on the surface, preventing evaporation of the solvents and giving it time to cut into the paint below.

The instructions for each type paint remover give the approximate time it takes to work. Test from time to time with your finger to see if it has cut through. This means all the way through to bare wood. Don't get eager and start to scrape before the solvent has had time to work through. There are times, however, when the solvents evaporate before they have time to cut through all the layers of paint or varnish, in which case, scrape off everything that will come easily and apply a second coat of remover.

If the remover is the water washable type, you won't need a scraper. Use coarse steel wool and a garden hose. When the finish has softened down to the wood, give it a blast of water and rub with the steel wool. It will wash away with relative ease. If the solvents did not cut through before evaporating out of the remover, you'll have to apply another coat. The liberal use of water makes it advisable to work out of doors whenever possible. Temperature needn't be a factor, except to you working, because the best removers work fine even at the freezing point. In fact, in warm weather they tend to evaporate more quickly, even though they work just as well up until they do evaporate.

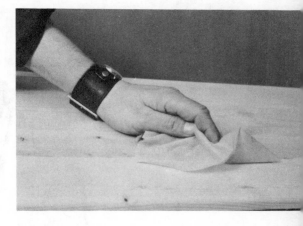

When wood is stripped bare and sanded, remove dust with rag soaked in turpentine or a tack rag, as described in the text. Brushing puts dust in air to mar the finish later.

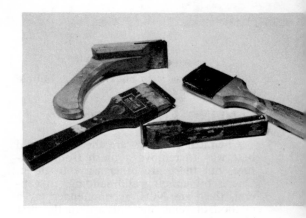

Scrapers of the type NOT recommended for most stripping operations. They are too big and sharp and will invariably gouge or nick wood, requiring some tedious repairs later.

When the piece stripped with water-washable remover is clean, let it dry completely before proceeding to the sanding stage.

Veneered furniture should never be stripped with water washable removers because the water will soften the veneer

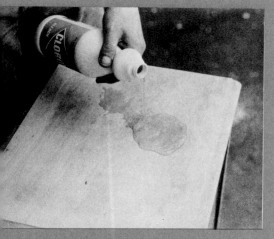

After stripping and sanding if the wood is still too dark to please you, it is easy to bleach. Ordinary laundry bleach is perhaps cheapest and effective enough for most jobs.

Solvents for shellac and lacquer are easy way to remove them. Just pour onto the surface, wait a minute and rub in with steel wool. When soft, wipe the old finish off.

glue and cause it to buckle, warp, bubble or come completely off.

SANDING AND SCRAPING

Chemical strippers are the easiest and best way to remove a finish from furniture, but there are other ways to do it. One is by scraping and sanding. In general, they are NOT recommended as a method of removing finishes. In the first place, they require a lot of muscle, even when you use an electric sander. And in the second place, they can ruin the wood surface of the piece you are working on. If it is a fine piece of furniture sanding and scraping will remove enough wood to ruin the fine surface already there. And if it is an antique, sanding and scraping will remove the antique surface of the wood, destroying its color, patina and signs of age which label it as authentic.

The proper place for mechanical means of paint removing such as sanding and scraping is in the touch up after you have used a chemical paint remover.

There will almost always be bits of old paint and varnish left in corners and crevices which are easier to get with a scraper and a corner of sandpaper than any other way. Sanding or scraping may also be appropriate when stripping the finish in a limited area and you do not want to risk slopping paint remover onto an adjacent finish that is good.

The main thing to remember about mechanical methods of paint removal is that they are severe solutions to a problem that is best solved other ways. This has nothing to do with sanding wood to a fine surface in preparation for a new finish, of course. That will be covered in the next chapter.

WHAT TO DO ABOUT STAIN AND FILLER

Underneath the finish you are removing is almost certain to be stain and perhaps wood filler. You have a choice: you can take it or leave it.

If you like the color of the wood as

previously finished, you may elect to leave as much stain in as possible. If so, do not use the water washable paint removers. They take away a lot of stain and filler, especially the newer water soluble analine dye stains. Use a paint remover without water and watch carefully as you work to control the amount of stain being taken away so the wood will not become mottled. If it does, use more remover in spots to even up the color.

If you want to re-stain the wood to your own satisfaction, then go ahead and remove all the stain and varnish with a water washable paint remover. There may be spots in which not all of the stain is taken away but they can be evened up with ordinary laundry chlorine bleach.

HEAT AS A STRIPPING AGENT

High heat will cause paint and varnish to curl up, blister, wrinkle, bubble and soften so you can easily scrape it off. When you use the right heat source, this is an acceptable method of stripping, although there is seldom any need for it.

Do not use a gas torch or any heat source with open flame. You run a high risk of starting a fire and/or ruining the piece of furniture you're trying to save. Besides there are better heat sources. One is a special commercial heat applicator which can be purchased or rented at many larger paint supply stores. They are little more than electric heating coils with a long handle. For more limited heat stripping, such as nooks and crannies missed by the chemical agents, you can use a soldering iron. Some of the new soldering guns have special wide tips which work well for this job.

The penetrating power of heat is often limited and where there are many layers of paint, only the top layer or two will be affected. Some people believe that the best combination for removing multi-layers of paint is to get off the top layers with heat and the lower layers with chemical removers. This avoids the danger of charring the wood, of course. But it is really easier and cheaper (unless you already own a heat appliance) to use chemical paint removers for the entire undertaking.

On vertical surfaces, use one of the paint removers with thickeners designed to make it stick. Apply as usual with brush, remove with scraper or brush. Wash surface clean.

Rubber gloves protect hands from harsh chemicals of paint removers when scouring old paint off with coarse steel wool. Many people don't need gloves. Most, however, do.

Milk paint is found at the bottom of many layers of paint on some colonial antiques and it's impervious to commercial strippers. Try ammonia, from bottle, and steel wool.

Home-made paint remover is very effective but must be used carefully. Pour can of plumbing lye into quart of water and add corn starch to thicken. Use disposable mop.

SHELLAC AND VARNISH

Just to remind you, you don't need paint removers of any kind for these finishes. They soften in their own solvents—alcohol for shellac and lacquer thinner for lacquer. Simply spread the solvent on evenly with a brush, wait until the finish softens, and wipe off with a solvent-soaked cloth. Follow up with another light brushing with solvent and another wiping, this time with a clean cloth. Since these solvents evaporate quickly, work only a small area at a time and check frequently to make sure the finish doesn't harden up again before you can wipe it clean.

Urethane, epoxy and other new finishes may be immune to the action of commercial paint removers. They were designed to achieve a very high degree of chemical resistance.

Stripping one of these finishes will probably require heat. Although any concentrated heat will do the job, open flame is not desirable because of the real danger of fire. An electrically heated paint remover such as is made by Red Devil will do the job best. And you can rent or buy one in most localities.

Sanding will also do the job, of course, but it is a lot of work and it removes too much wood to be desirable on fine furniture surfaces.

WAX AND OIL FINISHES

Often a piece of furniture will be finished with just wax or linseed oil. These must be removed before any other finish can be applied.

A linseed oil finish should be handled just as if it were varnish. Apply a good paint remover, let it work its alloted time and wash or scrape the residue away.

A wax finish is another story, however. Turpentine or mineral spirits will dissolve the wax, of course, if it can be reached. But when the wax has penetrated into the wood fibers, especially in the end grain, it will probably remain undissolved. And if there is any wax left on, a varnish finish will not harden. Therefore, remove as much wax as you can chemically, scrape and sand away as much more as possible and then seal the rest with shellac.

MILK PAINT

There is a kind of antique paint not used in the past 100 or so years known as "milk paint". The name is appropriate since it was made with milk solids and is chemically akin to casein glue. And just about as hard to get off. It is virtually immune to commercial paint removers, lye, trisodium phosphate, alcohol and lacquer thinner.

Chances are you'll find milk paint at the bottom of a number of layers. It is

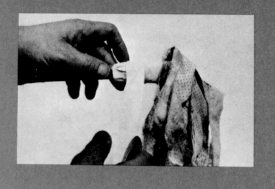

Homemade mop for applying lye-type paint remover is made from shredded piece of cloth which is then taped to a stick. Wear rubber gloves when working with remover.

Lye is neutralized with vinegar and water. Scrub down piece after it is scraped clean to stop the chemical action. Keep water and vinegar handy when working as precaution.

probably the original paint and therefore deserves consideration. Especially if it is decorated, it may be worth as much as the piece of furniture. Consider stripping the top layers of paint and retaining the milk paint. It can be restored somewhat and may be interesting and pretty.

Ammonia is the secret of removing milk paint. Plain, undiluted household ammonia, just as it comes from the bottle. Pour a cup full into a bowl and dip a pad of coarse steel wool in it. Then scrub at the milk paint with it. Keep dipping and scrubbing until the entire paint surface is wet. Keep it wet with ammonia for at least 10 minutes. Finally, the paint will start to decompose rapidly and can be wiped or scraped away. But you must keep wetting down the paint.

Warning—ammonia produces dangerous fumes and should be used out of doors or in a well ventilated room. Since it is hard on the skin, wear rubber gloves and have a large bucket of clean water nearby to wash away any splashes that get on clothing or skin. Also wear the oldest clothing you can find.

LYE AS PAINT REMOVER

Lye is strong stuff and it frightens many people away from using it as a paint remover. It deserves respect, but if used properly it is safe and effective. In fact, it is the most effective paint stripper available to most people. It will cut through three or four layers of heavy paint in five or ten minutes. The big drawback in using lye, other than personal safety, is that it stains wood dark.

Purchase lye at a hardware, paint or plumbing supply store where it is sold as a plumbing drain cleaner. It is important that you read the cautions on the label. Lye will burn the skin after a few seconds contact and can cause blindness in the eyes. So always have a large bucket of water handy and at least a quart of vinegar as a neutralizer. Use rubber gloves.

Mix one can of lye to a quart of water. Always put the water in the bucket first and then add the lye. It will have a vigorous reaction and appear to be boiling. The water will become quite hot. Never put the lye in first and add water to it. The reaction will be violent. Another precaution: do not use aluminum in conjunction with lye because the metal reacts with the lye to produce a deadly gas. It is also dangerous to use plastic containers because the heat of the lye reaction.

If you intend to use the lye paint remover on vertical surfaces, add cornstarch or wheat type wallpaper paste to thicken it—about one cup per gallon.

Once the lye paste is applied to the paint, check every minute or so to see how far it has cut into the paint. If you do not want it to reach the bare wood, stop its action at the last layer by washing it down with water and vinegar.

The type of finish you pick for your project depends on use as well as good looks. This dining room table must be resistant to water and other liquids as well as to heat and scuffs.

PICKING THE BEST FINISH

Some finishes are best for beauty, some for wear and some for ease of application

Sometime between the process of cleaning up the stripped furniture piece and the time you do the final sanding of the wood, you have to face the decision of what kind of a finish to put on.

More than likely you have known from the start what kind of a look you want to achieve. Or you know that you want a finish which is rugged. Or you want something that's easy to put on. Which finish is best for what criteria? There are three things to keep in mind: LOOKS, TOUGHNESS and PROBLEMS OF APPLICATION.

Before analyzing these properties of finishes, let's look at the basic finishing materials that are available to the home craftsman.

TYPES OF FINISHES

The three old standbys are *shellac, varnish* and *lacquer. Enamel paint* is essentially varnish with color pigment in it. *Boiled linseed oil* can be used successfully as a finish although it is difficult to apply and not very serviceable. A very new type of finish, not always available in paint and hardware stores, is *penetrating finish* containing plastic material which soaks into the fibers of the wood and hardens to give the wood a durable protective surface that loods as if it were perfectly natural without any finish at all. There are also a wide variety of synthetic resins such as alkyds, vinyls and urethanes but these are generally just improvements on previous resins used in varnishes. *Wax is not a finish.* It is a wonderful way to protect a finish but should never be used on bare wood. It will soak into the wood fibers nicely and then absorb all kinds of dirt and impurities for years and be impossible to clean. The wax will be virtually impossible to remove without sanding the wood down drastically, and no finish will adhere over the wax.

THE LOOK

Each finishing job ends up with a "look". It's a very important thing, more art than science. Two refinishers can put on the same material in the same way, technically speaking, and come up with quite different "looks". One may be deep and full of character and the other plain and lusterless. Experience and experimentation will help you develop the "look" you want.

In trying to achieve the look you want, the first decision you have to make is fairly easy. Do you want a clear finish or an opaque color finish? Do you want it to look more or less like natural wood or do you want to cover it up with paint, enamel or colored lacquer?

Shellac, clear lacquer, varnish and penetrating resin are all more or less colorless and permit the wood grain to show through. Some shellacs and varnishes are rather dark and will make the wood much richer and darker. Clear lacquer, some synthetic-resin varnishes and penetrating resin are clear as water and have about the same darkening effect on wood as water.

Stand for marble-topped Victorian table takes on new life with a top coating. Since there is little wear or other abuse, even the more delicate finishes can be used in such applications.

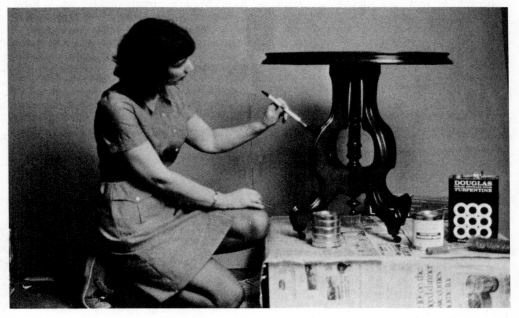

Former kitchen cupboard is promoted to formal dining room status by stripping to bare wood and applying practical and beautiful natural wood finish. Worth the trouble.

Some finishes, especially shellac, must be protected by a good coat of wax. It will buff up to a high gloss. Wax protects shellac from white spots caused by water spilled on tops.

For an opaque color finish, enamel and colored lacquer are most often used. Lacquer gives a harder, crisper surface than enamel, in general, but there are ways of applying enamel to achieve a lacquer look. With opaque finishes, no wood grain shows through, of course.

TONE AND COLOR

The next decision to make is on the tone or color of the project. For an opaque finish such as enamel or lacquer, it's relatively simple: look at a color chart, or mix pigments to get the exact color you want. For transparent natural finishes it's a bit more complicated.

Quite frequently the natural color of the wood will not be to your liking. Plain, unstained pine, for example, is quite white with very little grain showing. Yet Scandanavian and Japanese furniture is often finished with the unstained. But for the rich, grainy "early-American" look, pine is always stained a warm brown. There is a wide range of commercial wood stains, approximating the color of all the common types of wood such as

oak, walnut, mahogany, pine, cherry and so on. These may be used to heighten the grain of their namesake woods, or used on other woods to achieve a special effect. They can also be mixed, as long as you stick to the same type of stain. There are stains to match every possible color.

Some stains penetrate into the fibers of the wood while others build up on the surface. Some stains are applied before the finish while others are contained in the finish itself. Some stains are water based, some are alcohol based and some are oil based. Which to use depends on the wood, its condition, ease of application, the type of finish going over it and other things. See the chapter on "Staining" for specific characteristics of each.

Some times you may want to make the wood lighter. This calls for bleaching. Often, plain laundry bleach will lighten the wood sufficiently. If not, use a two-part bleach available at larger paint supply stores or the mail-order craftsman supply houses. There are also lacquer lighteners which are both finish and lightener together.

A penetrating resin finish was used on this old bench to leave the wood looking as natural as possible, yet give it protection against stains and the usual physical wear.

Another use of penetrating resin finish on an old side table. Since this type finish leaves the wood looking bare and natural, the stripping and sanding must be done with care.

TEXTURE

Texture is an important and often neglected aspect of a finish. In most finishes you see on furniture, something has been done to modify the natural texture of the wood. Yet with certain woods such as teak, the texture is so pleasing that it is invariably left natural and only sealed with a penetrating finish.

Your decision then is whether to leave the texture of the wood natural or to make the wood as smooth as possible with a filler. The type of finish you use will, to some extent, be influenced by which way you go on texture. A natural texture calls for a thin finish such as penetrating resin or perhaps clean lacquer. A smooth texture with the wood pores filled calls for a built up finish such as shellac, varnish or brushing lacquer.

A filler is just a paste or a cream-consistancy liquid which is brushed over the wood filling the pores. When it starts to set up, the surface is wiped clean, leaving the hardened substance in the pores. A filler can be obtained to match the stain used or built into the stain. Or the filler can be a contrasting value or even a color. With open grained woods such as oak, chestnut, walnut or mahogany, fillers are frequently used. Sometimes the pores are filled with color filler for novelty effects as is occasionally seen on oak. Fine grained woods like pine, birch, maple, cherry and beach do not require fillers.

The effect of a filler is to make the wood perfectly smooth. The finish is then built up on top to give it depth and gloss. Wood left in its natural state of texture is usually given a thin, penetrating finish.

93

GLOSS

If you've decided on a natural texture for the wood and a thin penetrating finish to seal and harden it, there is no question of gloss. The wood will look as if no finish had been applied. If you have decided to fill the wood pores, or if the wood is close grained, you have a choice on the build up and sheen of the finish. It may be thick and glassy or thin and flat. Or any combination of thickness and glossiness.

For a high gloss, varnish may be the easiest finish to work with. There are varnishes which develop a satin sheen right out of the can. The only problem here is with dust. Varnish takes from 8 to 24 hours to dry hard enough to recoat, and four hours to set hard enough so it won't be affected by dust. But in a dust-laden atmosphere, the finish can be ruined in a few minutes.

Both shellac and lacquer can be polished to a high gloss and they dry so quickly that dust is not a big problem. They are applied in many coats, with much polishing in between. In this way a deep, rich, high-gloss finish can be achieved. Of course, varnish can be polished too with a second and third coat to achieve the depth of finish you want. Materials for polishing in-between coats are extra fine sandpaper, rottenstone and various grades of pumice, the latter two generally used with water or oil.

Opaque color finishes can be treated like varnish with polishing in-between coats to achieve a lacquer-like finish. The final look, whether very glossy or a flat matte finish, can be rubbed on with appropriate abrasive materials.

TOUGHNESS

Varnish and urethane finishes are tough. Shellac can be fragile. Either can be built up in depth or applied thinly. What you use depends on the use to which the furniture piece will be put. On a cocktail table, shellac would be almost a disaster, for example. Shellac will dissolve in anything from alcohol to hard water. But on a beautiful chair that is little used, shellac may be the best possible

Penetrating resin is flowed liberally on legs and stretchers and allowed to soak in before wiping. For better penetration, legs can be turned to horizontal plane for application

Penetrating resin finish can be applied with brush or soft cloth. It is allowed to soak in until wood pores are full and then wiped off with a cloth leaving color unchanged

Epoxy finish is extremely tough. A chemical hardener is added just before use to make the finish cure chemically instead of through evaporation. It is almost clear and glossy.

Texture of the beautiful wood in this end table cabinet is preserved by the finish which is nevertheless elegantly glossy. Lacquer provides this beauty and protection.

finish because of its ease of application, high resistance to abrasion and flexing and the fact that it can be built up into any number of highly polished coats. In addition, a shellac finish can very easily be touched up when marred.

Varnish is tough and most people like its look on furniture. The big problem is length of drying time. As stated earlier, this characteristic makes it subject to dust spots. Varnish can be applied in thin coats like lacquer and shellac and polished in between for a high gloss finish.

Varnish is highly resistant to alcohol, water and most common chemicals but it is not highly resistant to abrasion and flexing. Furniture which must undergo great differences in temperature may develop fine cracks or even chipping in the varnish finish. But all in all, varnish is the finish that most furniture refinishers find to be the best combination of good looks and durability, despite the problems of application.

Lacquer is similar to shellac in application and durability. Of the big three finishes, it darkens wood the least and it can be applied the fastest. The danger is in lacquer drying too fast. Spraying lacquer, used on most commercial furniture, dries in seconds and is not recommended for home refinishing since it cannot be applied with a brush. There are excellent brushing lacquers which set up in a matter of minutes. The advantage of this property is that many layers of lacquer can be built up in a day. It can be polished between layers, of course, to build up a high gloss finish. Lacquer provides excellent protection for the wood in terms of abrasion and resistance to water but it is brittle and may chip or crack in applications where the wood flexes.

Of the many new synthetic finishes on the market, the penetrating finish alone constitutes a new category. It soaks into the wood fibers and cures without affecting the wood visually at all and yet it provides resistance to moisture, chemicals, stains and wear. Of the synthetic resin varnishes, there are acrylics, vinyls, polyurethanes, silicons, epoxies and others available now. In general, however, they are improvements on previous varnishes which were already vastly superior to most transparent finishes.

Orbital power sanders are okay for large, flat surfaces. Use hand power on edges.

PREPARING WOOD
FOR A NEW FINISH

Proper procedure is easy but very important: No finish is better than the wood

All procedures prior to this were aimed at getting the furniture project ready for a new finish. You should now have caught up with the original cabinetmaker at the finishing stage: a piece of furniture which is structurally sound but still bare wood, which may have minor dents and discolorations. So whether your project has been stripped down or is a piece of unpainted furniture or is something you made yourself, the procedure from here on is the same.

MINOR DENTS

Large dents and holes should have

been repaired before this stage, as described in an earlier chapter. Small dents have a way of happening while you are working and should be filled or removed at this stage. Plastic wood can be used for filling but it is better to remove the dent, either by sanding or by the ingenious use of moisture. Sanding is self-evident.

Moisture will often take away shallow dents. The dent was caused in the first place by compression of the wood fibers by some sort of blow. Application of moisture causes these compressed fibers to swell up again, usually to their original shape. The easiest way to apply moisture is to sprinkle a little water on the dents.

A few pin pricks in the dent will facilitate water reaching the fibers that need it.

If that doesn't work, try steaming. An ordinary clothes iron will do the job well. Place a damp cloth over the dent and apply the point of the iron, turned to the heat setting called "Cotton". Remove quickly before the wet cloth starts to scorch because if the wood is burned or scorched, you will be faced with the problem of severe discoloration. A heavy soldering iron will also do a fine job, although they usually do not have a positive heat control. The safest method to use with a soldering iron is to let it reach full heat, then unplug it and keep testing it on a spare damp cloth until it produces steam without burning or scorching. Keep wetting the cloth and applying heat until the dent disappears. You may have to do some light sanding to make it invisible.

Dents in wood can sometimes be removed by steaming. The compressed wood fibers expand with the moisture and eventually regain their original shape. An ordinary clothing iron and wet cloth will do the job.

DISCOLORED WOOD

Any discoloration in the wood will affect the final finish to some extent. Obviously a transparent lacquer finish will reveal the discolored area plainly, even with a clean stain over it. But also a discolored spot caused by grease or oil will prevent an opaque finish from adhering properly to the wood. The safest thing to do is remove them all. Here's how to remove some of the usual things.

Grease spots nearly come out with the application of either benzine or acetone. The former is best for animal grease, the latter for vegetable grease. Since you rarely know which kind of grease made the spot, try both. Commercial "spot" removers made for clothing also work well on most grease and oil spots in wood. Whichever type of remover you use, brush it on liberally, then sprinkle the area with corn meal to absorb both remover and grease. Brush away the corn meal after an hour or so. If some grease remains, repeat procedure.

Iron stains appear as black or gray streaks and spots in wood. Frequently it is in the area of a piece of hardware which got wet and ran onto the wood. These can usually be removed by an oxalic acid solution. Apply locally with an artists brush so as not to lighten the wood around it. If this happens, however, wash the entire surface of wood with oxalic

Stains in the wood caused by oxidizing iron or other metal can often be removed by a solution of oxalic acid and warm water. Apply with artists' brush and let soak. If wood gets too light, stain to original color.

acid solution to lighten it uniformly. It can be stained later. Then neutralize the action with vinegar or ammonia. Also try ordinary laundry bleach or hydrogen peroxide for some black spots.

General dinginess is often a problem especially with older pieces. The wood becomes gray, faded and lifeless. To rejuvenate the wood and restore some of the original color, wash the entire piece with laundry detergent and very hot water. Rinse and wipe as dry as possible. Then wash the piece again in a solution of very hot water and oxalic acid, mixed two ounces to the pint of water. Brush on liberally and let stand ten or fifteen minutes.

Hand scraper is sometimes best way to smooth badly scarred wood like this bed-table leg. Blade was set for very thin cut and it was pulled with the grain. Great care must be taken not to knick wood worse.

Glass is an effective and inexpensive scraper. A broken pane takes many shapes, one of which is likely to fit the shape of the work. When the glass edge gets dull, just move up a bit or rebreak the glass for new edge.

Six common grits of garnet paper used by refinishers. The grit range is from 6/0 to 1½. Some of the finer grades should be in both open and closed coats for situations where the sandpaper tends to load up excessively.

Rinse with water and neutralize the acid with ammonia or vinegar. It won't look like new wood, but it should have a nice, mellow look to it.

SCRAPING AND PLANING

At this stage, there should seldom be a need to plane or scrape the wood. This is always done by the original maker when he shapes the pieces before assembling them. However, once in a while some later event will damage a piece of furniture so badly that sanding may seem too slow and laborious. If you do decide to use a plane or scraper at this stage, use it sparingly and make sure the tool is very sharp. A dull blade will rough up the surface badly, perhaps incurably. Both plane and scraper do the same thing—remove wood from the surface. Scrapers just remove less.

Of the many types of scrapers available, the best are homemade. These are just a piece of hard sheet steel (like an old saw blade) squared off with a file and burnished to make an almost microscopic hook along the cutting edge. This type scraper is held in both hands, almost vertical to the plane of the wood surface, and drawn toward you lightly. At the end of a board, scrape inward, turning the scraper so the vertical plane is at an angle to the direction of draw. If you draw from the center of the board over the edge, there is a danger of splitting off too much wood.

Commercial scrapers such as are used to remove paint from exterior walls of houses are not appropriate for furniture work.

Excellent scrapers can be made from broken glass. Select the shape to match the wood surface and use it as described

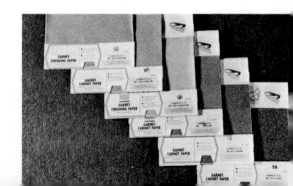

This enlarged view of sandpaper grit material shows some of the differences. In order they are flint, garnet, aluminum oxide and emery. The last is used mostly in metalworking and not often used in wood finishing.

This enlarged photograph shows the difference in size of the various grits of garnet. From top left, clockwise, is grit #½, 2/0, 4/0 and 6/0. The 6/0 grit is about the finest used by refinishers. Finer grits are available.

above. When the sharp edge becomes dull, break it again to create a new edge.

You can also make or buy curved metal scrapers which are burnished with a slightly hooked edge and are used for moldings, carvings and other non-flat areas.

A smoothing plane may be used on surfaces where the grain is fairly straight and not reversed. Otherwise, the plane blade will dig big chunks out of the wood and ruin the surface. Use the smallest plane you have that is appropriate to the size of the job. Make certain the face of the plane is clean and rust-free so you don't discolor the surface. Set the bite of the blade as small as possible and increase it as necessary while you work.

"SANDING"

This headline is in quotes because the one abrasive material not used in smoothing wood is sand. Even so-called sandpaper is surfaced with an abrasive of considerably higher quality than sand. Before going into the techniques of sanding, let's look at the types of "sandpaper" available to the home craftsman. Things to consider are (1) type of abrasive, (2) size of grit, (3) density of abrasive and (4) backing material. First, there are five types of abrasives in general use. Only three of them are suitable for woodworking projects although one of the most unsuitable, flint paper, is widely used, probably because it is cheap. But flint paper is an extravagance because it is the most ineffective.

TYPE OF ABRASIVE

1. **Flint paper.** This is the oldest woodworking abrasive, the traditional sandpaper. Its continuing popularity is due to low price and habit. There is nothing in performance which makes it worthwhile. It is a natural material with poor cutting and poor lasting qualities.

2. **Emery.** This is the blue-black cloth-backed abrasive that is sometimes thought to be best for metalworking. It is not. The natural mineral from which it is made does not possess sufficient cutting characteristics and so it really should be thought of as a polishing material. There is almost no excuse for it in woodworking projects, considering the other superior materials available.

3. **Garnet.** This is also a natural mineral abrasive with a reddish look to it. It is the best of the natural abrasives and the most used. It is reasonably hard and maintains a continuous cutting edge despite use. It is used both for smoothing raw wood and for between-coat polishing.

4. **Aluminum oxide.** This is an artificial abrasive and is both the toughest and most durable of the five common abrasives. In the finer grits, it has the best cutting qualities of all. Sold under trade names like *Adalox* and *Metalite*, aluminum oxide papers work equally well on wood or metal. It is reddish brown.

5. **Silicon Carbide.** This abrasive is also made from synthetic mineral material and is blue-black in color. It is extremely sharp and has a hardness approaching that of diamonds. This makes it excellent

Retail	Old Style	Industrial	Uses
Super Fine	—	600	Polishing metals, ceramics, stone and plastic; usually used wet. Not used for wood or wood finishes.
	—	500	
	10/0	400	
Extra Fine	9/0	360	
	—	320	
Very Fine	8/0	280	Polishing finishes between coats; usually used wet.
	7/0	240	
	6/0	220	
Fine	5/0	180	Finishing bare wood.
	4/0	150	
	3/0	120	
Medium	2/0	100	First sanding for soft woods. Shaping.
	1/0 or 0	80	
	½	60	
Coarse	1	50	Paint removal from furniture; rough sanding and shaping.
	1½	40	
Very Coarse	2	36	Machine sanding bare floors; first cut.
	2½	30	
	3	24	
Extra Coarse	3½	20	Machine sanding floors to remove paint and old coatings.
	4	16	
	4½	12	

for sanding hardwood floors, ceramics, glass, plastics and metal. Its uses in woodworking extend from coarse shaping to between-coat polishing. Aluminum oxide papers can be used dry or wet, as with a light lubricating oil to create a satin finish.

COMPARATIVE SIZE OF ABRASIVE GRITS

All of the abrasive materials listed above are available in a wide range of grit sizes. These sizes are graded by three different systems. Since a home woodworker may run into any one of them, they are all listed here so you can compare one to another. The grit size number or description is always printed on the backing paper of cloth. And the systems apply to all sandpaper, regardless of the abrasive materials, although there may be minor differences. For example, a grit size which is labelled "Very Fine" on a garnet paper is called "Extra Fine" on flint paper.

OPEN-COAT AND CLOSE-COAT SANDPAPER

The performance of sandpaper is affected by other characteristics than type of abrasive and size of the grit grains. The *amount* of grit covering the backing paper or cloth is also important. In practice, there are two types of grit coverage. The most common type is called "Close-Coat" sandpaper and it has the abrasive material covering 100% of the backing. The second type is called "Open-Coat" sandpaper and it has abrasive material covering 50% to 70% of the backing.

Close-Coat sandpaper is the most generally used and it is ideal for hard woods and other hard material which will not "load" the abrasive. That is, the fine wood chips of hardwoods are less likely to lodge in between the grit grains and reduce the cutting power of the sandpaper. A Close-Coat sandpaper is best for the finer grit sizes and for achieving a fine finish.

Open-Coat sandpaper has spaces be-

Better quality sandpapers such as garnet and aluminum oxide grits have strong enough backing and glue that they can be washed out with solvent. Flint cannot be cleaned.

Sandpaper comes in a variety of backing materials as well as a variety of grit materials. Paper backings usually come in four weights, the lightest for working in crevices.

tween the grains of grit to prevent loading when used on softwoods and other soft materials. They leave tiny chips which tend to choke up Close-Coat sandpapers, but which either fall out of Open-Coat sandpapers, or can easily be knocked out.

It should be noted in passing that there is a distinct difference in the quality of sandpapers, even when they seem to have the same characteristics. This is due, in part, to the method of applying the grit to the backing material. The traditional method is by a gravity process using mechanical controls to guide the direction and flow of grit grains. It cannot produce enough uniformity for any but coarse-grained sandpapers, however.

To achieve the precise uniformity required for medium to super-fine grain sandpapers, especially for polishing finishes, the abrasive material is applied electrostatically. This is the process developed by the Norton abrasives people for their Bear brand sandpapers. It keeps the abrasive grains equi-distant apart throughout the sandpaper surface, and it keeps the sharpest point of each grain exposed for maximum cut.

Another area in which sandpaper quality differs is in the adhesive used to hold the grit to the backing material. For the cheap, light-duty and medium-duty sandpapers, animal hide glue is most often used. Sometimes this glue will be improved by the addition of chemicals to strengthen its holding power and increase its resistance to heat. The additives also improve the sandpapers' resistance to

shredding, compared to plain animal hide glue, making them superior for medium to light-heavy duty work.

For heavy-duty work such as shaping wood of sanding floors, thermo-setting resins are used, sometimes in conjunction with glue. The resins are waterproof and, when applied to waterproof backing material, can be used for wet sanding operations, using either water or oil. Most sandpapers have the designation "wet" or "Wet-or-dry" printed on the backing material. In all the important characteristics, resin adhesive is superior to any other used in sandpapers.

SANDPAPER BACKING MATERIALS

As we all know, sandpaper rarely contains sand and frequently does not have paper as a backing material. But the choice of the right backing is important. Characteristics such as flexibility, durability, water-resistance, heat resistance and cutting power are affected by the backing material. There are three backing materials in general use—paper, cloth and fiber—although the home craftsman will not be likely to encounter fiber which is used in metalworking production. There are also combinations of these materials, which do not apply to furniture refinishing.

Paper Backing—Four different paper backings are generally used for sandpaper and they are identified by weight, and usually labelled that way on the back.

"A-Weight"—this is the lightest, most pliable paper backing. It is used for finish-

Sanding belts and discs are used with power sanders. They are handy for rough work on some furniture but they remove too much to be used on fine furniture or antiques.

Turned parts of furniture should be sanded with the direction of the turning since it is almost impossible to sand with the grain. End with finest sandpaper you can buy.

Sand long flat surfaces with the grain always. Make long strokes with sanding block, rather than short, scrubby ones for a more uniform surface. Knock out dust to clean.

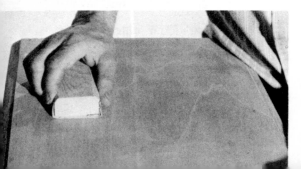

ing papers, those fine grits designed primarily for light hand sanding and finish sanding where flexibility is important and durability is not.

"C-Weight"—this paper backing material is lightly stiffer and has more strength than "A-Weight". It is used for hand or light machine sanding operations. Generally it is used for Medium grit sandpapers.

"D-Weight"—just a trifle stiffer and stronger than "C-Weight" paper and is used for Medium to Coarse grit sandpapers. It is best for rough sanding by hand or machine.

"E-Weight"—this is the stiffest, strongest backing paper of all. Used principally for drum or belt sanding where the backing must have the strength to withstand severe sanding operations such as floors.

"Cloth Backing"—There are two grades, designated by letters on the back:

"J-Weight"—light and flexible, is used primarily for hand sanding and polishing, in the finer grades. "J" weight cloth is the standard backing for emery, as well.

"X-Weight"—a heavier, stronger cloth backing used primarily for heavy-duty machine grinding operations. This weight is often rather specialized and sold under specific trade names such as Nortons' *Adalox*.

Fiber and Combination Backings — Laminated cellulose fiber, sometimes combined with heavy duty drill cloth, is used as backing for large, heavy-duty industrial grinding discs which are used primarily in metalworking operations. Paper-cloth combinations are used for floor sanding where extreme flexibility is not necessary but resistance to tearing is.

SANDING TECHNIQUES

As stated several times before, the final finish cannot be better than the wood surface you achieve under it. If the wood has dents, scratches or unevenly sanded surface, it will show up in the final finish. In fact, you may very well find it is impossible to get the finish you want in the end.

Sanding wood smooth is simplicity itself. It doesn't require expensive tools and you don't have to expend a great

amount of labor. But there are a few simple steps which are required to get the degree of uniform smoothness you need.

The basic rule is: never sand more than necessary and never sand less than necessary. Sounds simple but finishers just seem to sand without paying attention to the results they get. For example, some inexperienced refinishers start with sandpaper that is too coarse for the job. Or they progress to sandpaper that is finer than the wood responds to. Start sanding with the finest grit that will cut the wood quickly and still make it smoother than when you started. And when you get to a grit that doesn't seem to be making it any smoother, stop. When you're there, you're there.

Another rule is: always sand with the grain. Cross cuts have a pernicious way of showing up in the final finish, especially if it is clear. Once you make a scratch across the grain, it is a lot of work to sand it out again. The only exception is with wood turnings and carvings. These are often impossible to sand with the grain. If you use "A" weight paper and end up with the finest grade steel wool, the surface will be satisfactory. This is partly because the curved surfaces do not show blemishes as readily as mirror smooth flat surfaces.

Enlarged photo shows how coarse grit sandpaper affects the wood. This is actually too rough for any furniture. Compare it with the photo below showing effect of fine grade.

Fine grade sandpaper produces a surface like this on a piece of white pine. It was preceded by coarse and medium grades. Next smooth with extra fine, followed by wetting.

SANDING BLOCKS

For flat surfaces, some kind of sanding block is a necessity. For curved edges a sanding block is also very desirable. If you try to sand a large area with light weight sandpaper against your hand or fingers, the grit simply rides down into the soft, low areas, gouging them deeper. And the high spots are not cut down sufficiently. The result will be a wavy surface. Curved edges that are sanded without a block tend to get rounded corners.

You can make a sanding block that is as good as, or better than any you can buy, as far as the results can be seen in the finish. Every paint store carries types of commercial sanding blocks. Some have rolls of sandpaper which you uncoil as you use it up. Others have patented clamping systems to hold the sandpaper

in place and are often more work to change the sandpaper than to hold it in the first place. They are made of wood, plastic, metal and have pads of rubber, plastic, cloth or no padding at all.

As everyone knows, it's easy to make a sanding block. It usually consists of rummaging through the scrap bin until you find a suitable piece of wood. Place the sandpaper over it and hold the edges with your fingers and start sanding. There is one serious drawback and one not-so-serious drawback to this kind of home-

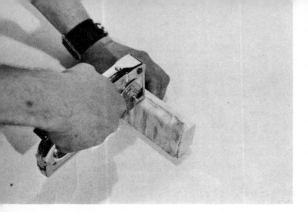

Sanding blocks are easy to make. Always use semi-firm padding between block and the sandpaper to prevent excess loading and wear spots. An old felt hat brim is good.

Commercial sanding blocks are available at almost all hardware stores. Some, like this one, do not have padding so it must be added. Lever on handle actuates grippers.

Curved sanding blocks should be made for sanding curved surfaces. This one, for sanding edges is cut to a variable radius so some portion of the curve will fit any section.

made block. The second, not-so-serious, drawback is that it's uncomfortable to hold. Hollow out the sides slightly for a better grip and round the back slightly and you can hold the paper more comfortably. The serious drawback is that sandpaper against a bare block ruins sandpaper quicker and does not do a better job than a padded block. The bare block causes the sandpaper grit to make contact only with the tops of ridges of the work being sanded, causing excess friction and loading up the sandpaper too fast. With a thin pad between sandpaper and block the grit makes contact slightly on either side of the ridges, thereby taking away more wood without pin-pointing the friction.

To pad the sanding face of the block, use the felt from the brim of an old hat. If you don't have one, use ordinary store-bought felt or even a couple of layers of heavy cloth such as worn denim. This padding can be tacked in place along the edges but it works better when secured with Elmers' glue. Apply sparingly so it won't soak through and make a hard spot, which will make scratches.

The size of the face of the sanding block is not very important except that it should be some multiple of the size of a full sheet of sandpaper. Since most sandpaper comes in 9″ by 11″ sheets, you can cut eight pieces that are 4½″ by 2¾″. Since you'll need at least ¼″ overlap of the sandpaper for gripping, you can use a block that is 4½″ by 2¼″ or 4″ by 2¾″. This is an often used size but larger pieces can be used, say six or even four per sheet.

SPECIAL SANDING BLOCKS

To sand long curved surfaces or curved edges, make special sanding blocks. An assortment of cylindrical shapes such as a short length of 1″ dowel, clothes rod or child's block all comes in handy as sanding blocks. Smaller sizes are especially helpful when sanding concave curved edges. Without any block, there is a danger of rounding the corners of the edge. For concave edges and surfaces, it is often best to plane a block to the specific radius and use it with appropriate padding.

For convex surfaces, carve out the center of the sanding block to the same approximate radius. For convex edges, a concave sanding block can be cut with bandsaw or saber saw. As always, they should be used with padding.

WHICH GRIT TO USE, AND WHEN

Start with the finest sandpaper which will do the job. For most refinishing projects and even unpainted furniture, your entire sandpaper inventory need not be coarser than 2/0 which is in the range called "Fine". Yes, that means you probably will not need "Medium" or "Coarse" grades for the final smoothing operations. These are for rough sanding and shaping wood.

On hardwoods and most softwoods, a 3/0 grade sandpaper (also known as "Fine" and "120" grit) is suitable to start with. You may find the extra cutting power of 2/0 best for some softwoods, however. Use all sandpaper with a padded sanding block, of course.

SANDING STROKES

The importance of even strokes and an equal number of strokes cannot be overemphasized. It can make a great deal of difference in the final finish, especially if it is a clean natural finish. When sanding, use a firm but not heavy pressure. Learn to do it naturally, without thinking, so that it never varies from one part of the furniture piece to another.

Be sure to give each area of the project approximately the same number of sanding strokes. Count them if you have to. Because the way stain and finishing materials look on the wood will vary slightly according to the amount of sanding, even though both areas feel equally smooth.

FINER GRITS

After the first sanding with 2/0 or 3/0 garnet paper, switch to a finer grade. Whether you go to the final grade or to an intermediate grade depends on the wood and the finish you intend to put on it. For softwood like pine you can proba-

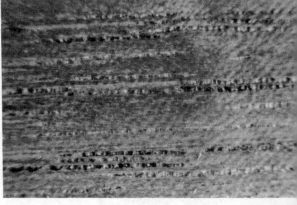

Wood fibers enlarged many times show grain and tiny pores. The grain must be smoothed and the pores filled for a smooth level finish. Fibers are raised with water.

Enlarged photo of wood grain shows fibers standing up. This was done by wetting the wood so, when dry, they can be knocked off with extra fine sandpaper until smooth.

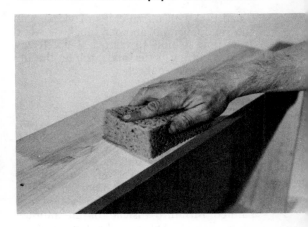

bly go right to a 6/0 sandpaper. For a hardwood like cherry, you will save a little work by using an intermediate grade, say 4/0 or 5/0. On any wood, if your final finish is to be enamel there is no point in going to any grade finer than 5/0 since the pigment in the paint will smooth it out anyway. On hardwood that is to get a clear finish, however, it may profit by working up to 7/0 or 8/0 grit.

To get more mileage out of your sandpaper, use one of the better abrasives such as garnet and, as it begins to fill, or

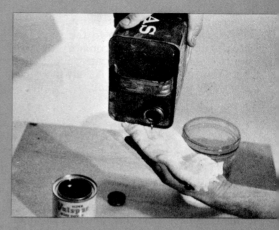

A tack rag is one of the best ways to remove dust and dirt prior to putting on a finish. Gummy substances in cloth pick up particles without marring or staining surface.

Tack rag ingredients are water, turpentine and a clear finish, in this case varnish. Cheese cloth is first soaked in water, then turpentine, to retard drying of the varnish.

"load up" with micro chips of wood, slap the sandpaper on another block of wood from time to time to remove them. It will keep it cutting better and prolong the life of the sandpaper sheet.

SANDING ANTIQUES

Perhaps most of the value of an antique is in the look of it. . . the color and patina which just happened over the years. That look is only about as deep as the paper these words are printed on. And overenthusiastic sanding can remove it. Then you have an old piece of unpainted furniture instead of an antique. So go lightly. Antiques don't need much sanding anyway, as a rule.

Another boo boo caused by too-heavy sanding is blotchiness. The old color has only been sanded away in a few places. If a new stain is applied over this, it will have a mottled or blotchy appearance. And it is almost impossible to stain the bare spots to match the original stain. At that point, about all you can do is cover the whole surface with a heavy stain, or remove it all to bare wood. Better to take it easy with the sanding block in the first place.

SUPER SMOOTHING WITH WATER AND SEALER

There comes a point when sanding any wood surface when it just won't get any smoother. When you go to finer grades of sandpaper, all you do is raise a fine fuzz of wood fibers. There are two things you can do to continue the smoothing operation. Wet the surface and/or use a sanding sealer.

Wetting the sanded surface causes the wood fibers to swell and raise tiny micro fibers. When the surface is absolutely dry again, resand with the last grade sandpaper used. This will knock off the standup fibers. Water treatment is especially important if you intend to use a water stain on the wood later because the water in the stain would only raise the fibers anyway. And at that point sanding tends to change the color of the stain slightly. But the fibers, once swollen, will not do much swelling the second time.

Wood surfaces can be made even smoother by using a sanding sealer. This is simply a thin wash of shellac, lacquer or varnish, much diluted in its own thinner (about 3 or 4 to 1). It is applied with a brush and the liquid causes the fibers to

Wring out water first, then add turpentine and wring out again. Then drip just enough varnish onto cheese cloth to make it evenly gummy throughout. Dust, dirt stick to rag.

Keep tack rags in jar with lid to keep them from drying out. Alternate method of making one is with water, raw linseed oil and shellac. Dampen in water, add shellac, oil.

swell and raise, just as water did. But when the sanding sealer is dry, the thin finish which has soaked into the wood hardens, setting the fibers more or less permanently. It can then be sanded with the last grit used and resanded with finer grits so an extremely smooth surface is achieved.

If the wood surface is to have a stain or wood filler, the sanding sealer should be applied after they are. Stains and wood filler will be discussed in more detail in the next chapter but briefly certain stains must penetrate the wood fibers in order to produce their intended colors. A sanding sealer, as the name implies, tends to retard this penetration of stains. Wood fillers are creamy or paste-like concoctions which will the open pores of certain types of wood to produce an absolutely smooth surface. They are applied after the stain and before any sanding sealer in order to assure a more perfect bond. Otherwise the filler may tend to chip.

As mentioned, you can make your own sanding sealer by diluting some clear finish to near water-like consistency with its own thinner. Special sanding sealers are sold under that name and claim to work just as well, regardless of the type of finish going over it.

DUSTING

As you sand you raise a dust of wood particles. It is important to keep this dust down as much as possible, especially if you intend to apply the finish in the same room later. And of course you don't do it in a room where another piece of furniture is being finished.

One of the best ways to control sanding dust is with a vacuum cleaner. Use the furniture brush and vacuum the surface after every stage of the sanding.

Another method of dust control is to use a tack rag. This can be purchased from a paint dealer or made at home by soaking cheesecloth in warm water, squeezing dry and adding turpentine liberally. Wring dry again, spread the cloth out and drip varnish all over. Roll and fold up and knead until varnish is distributed throughout. The resulting tack rag will be tacky and pick up dust without leaving any varnish behind. Keep in a sealed jar so it won't dry out when not in use.

Side table is stained to bring out grain. Then high gloss finish is applied to harden wood.

STAINS AND BLEACHES

Rarely does new wood look the way you'd like. A stain or bleach will change that

Just because a piece of furniture has been repaired, stripped to bare wood and sanded uniformly smooth all over, it does not mean that it's ready for the final finish. If you want a "natural" finish, that is, clear with wood grain showing through you will probably have to change the color of the raw wood. The natural look of wood is not what most people call "natural".

There are a variety of types and colors of wood stain available but they all accomplish one or more of three things: 1. they make new wood look older; 2. they help make one kind of wood match another; 3. they make the wood more beautiful by heightening color and bringing out the grain.

Sometimes, however, you may want to do the opposite. That is bleach the wood

very light or white and still have some grain showing through. Depending on how you accomplish this lightening process, it is called bleached, blonde, limed or pickled. At one time blonde finishes were very popular on Scandanavian furniture. Before that, it was popular on oak furniture. Today, it is popular on some Japanese pieces, even including bleached pine.

TYPES OF STAIN

Any material which changes the color of wood is called a stain. Sometimes it is not a good stain, as when a rusty nail stains wood. Copper sulfate will turn most woods almost black, which is good or bad depending on what your aim is. Potassium permangenate such as is used in photo processing will make many woods turn a

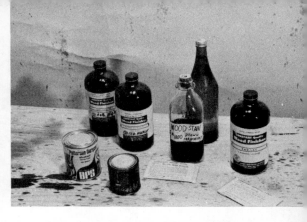

Comparison of the same piece of wood with and without stain showing how the grain is brought out beautifully. Different types of stain vary effect. You can lighten or darken.

Four of the most popular types of wood stain: wiping stain; water stain; non-grain-raising and all-in-one type stain containing a finishing coat. Choose type to suit project.

rich, aged brown. These home-made stains are used successfully every day by finishing experts. But they are difficult to predict and control. The home craftsman is better off using one of the many commercially available stains. There are three main types of stain, two of which are largely undiscovered by do-it-yourselfers. In addition, there are many unusual types of stain, most of which are of no use to home craftsmen.

Wiping Stain—This is the type of stain most people get when they ask for "stain" at the local paint store. It is also called "Pigmented Wiping Stain", "Penetrating Wiping Stain", "Glaze" and "Oil Stain", although you almost never find a true oil stain, which is rarely desirable.

Wiping stains such as *Miniwax, Benwood Stain,* and *Sapolin Wood Stain* contain a penetrating sealer in addition to color pigments. Penetrating sealers are usually synthetic resins which penetrate wood fibers and seal and harden them against further changes. A penetrating sealer will be virtually invisible in the wood when they do not contain pigments. Since these sealers prevent further staining, it is usually better to apply a wiping stain first and the sealer as a separate coat. Clear penetrating sealers are sold as Firzite, Clear Rez and Clear Miniwax, to name three.

A pigmented wiping stain does not work by penetrating the fibers of the

wood. It actually contains color pigments in suspension, which is why it must be stirred constantly as you work. Because the soft areas of the wood absorb more of the vehicle faster, there is more pigment deposited in the soft areas. And in scratches and cracks, which is great if you are trying for the "distressed" look. Soft woods like pine respond spectacularly to wiping stain, with the grain standing out very prominently. Other soft woods without such pronounced grain just soak up the wiping stain and get very dark. That's another reason why it's essential to test before each staining job. Close grained hardwoods do not respond well to wiping stains since little will soak in. If you leave it too long, it's just like muddy looking paint, that won't wipe off.

Pigmented wiping stains come in all the standard wood colors and in black, white and rainbow colors as well. They can be diluted or mixed to make intermediate shades. They do not raise the grain of the wood but, compared to the analine dye stains below, they are muddy and lack clarity and brilliance.

Non-Grain-Raising Stain—This type is a true dye, just like that used on cloth, which penetrates into and changes the color of the wood fibers. These analine dyes are included in petroleum derivative liquids which do not cause the wood fibers to swell and raise up. Hence, they are called "Non-Grain-Raising" or NGR.

Water stains are inexpensive and effective and they come in a wide variety of colors. Purchased as powder and mixed with water.

Non-grain-raising, or NGR, stains should always be purchased with an equal amount of its own compatible dilutant to lighten it.

Because NGR stains dry so fast, they are popular with furniture manufacturers. But they are difficult to get at local paint stores. They can be ordered from mail-order craftsman-supply houses, such as Constantine's. When you order, get the right thinner with it, since the color of the wood is controlled by thinning the stain and not by wiping it off.

Water Stain—This does not mean the alkali stain left by hard water. It is an analine dye stain, virtually the same as the NGR stain except that the vehicle is water. And water will cause wood fibers to swell and stand up. If the wood was wetted and sanded during the initial smoothing process, however, there will be very little grain fibers left to stand up.

Water stain comes in powder form, in little packets. You dissolve the contents in a quart of almost boiling water. It is generally applied hot or warm to increase penetration. Water stain come in all the standard wood colors, plus black and others such as red and green. Since any stain color will appear differently on different pieces of wood or even on different areas of the same piece, it is always best to test it first in some inconspicuous place. Wait until the stain is dry before judging color. If it turns out too dark, add more water. If it's too light, give it another staining, or heat up the stain and add more dye powder. If it is the wrong shade, blend in other dye powders, including black, red or

green, to get the color or shade you want.

The advantage of water stain is that it is the cheapest stain you can buy. (A one quart packet costs about 30 cents at Constantine's). They can also be used as the basis for your own NGR stains. Some types can be dissolved in denatured alcohol, which does not raise grain as much as water. Dyes in alcohol tend to be cooler in color than those dissolved in water. But either way, analine dyes give wood a clarity and brilliance of color that no other stain can match.

Varnish Stain—This is a low quality stain and finish combination used for the backs of furniture and other places where it will rarely be seen. It's just a blend of thin varnish and pigment.

Blending Stain—These are powdered stains which are applied raw, that is, without dissolving them in anything. They are applied with a soft pad soaked in special lacquer, usually sold as a Padding Lacquer. Blending stains are used over old finishes that have slight local damage. The pad is rubbed with the stain or stains that match the color of the original finish. Then rubbed into the damaged area until the match is perfect. Blending stains and padding lacquer are also used to cover an existing finish which is still good but not the precise color you want. Padding lacquer alone is not very durable but a top coat makes it long lasting.

Wiping stain is applied with brush or cloth and allowed to dry until it becomes dull on the surface. Wipe off surface when finished.

Final step in using wiping stain is to wipe glazed surface with cloth, turning frequently. Soft parts of wood hold more of the stain.

HOW TO APPLY STAINS

No matter what type of stain you use, the wood surface must be properly prepared, as mentioned earlier. It's too late, once staining begins, because further sanding will simply remove part of the stain work already done.

Before applying any stain, consider the effect it will have on the end grain (cut end) of the wood. End grain absorbs more stain faster than other surfaces, although the smoother it is sanded, the less tendency it will have to soak up stain. If you can test an inconspicuous end grain do so. To prevent over-darkening of end grain, apply a thin wash coat of shellac or sanding sealer. This will retard the absorption rate.

Applying a wiping stain—This type stain is so popular because it is simple and safe to apply. Since there are minor variations in each brand, always read the directions on the label for specific details. In general, wiping stain must be well stirred to keep the pigments in suspension. This usually includes a stir or two every five or ten minutes while you're working.

Apply the wiping stain evenly in long strokes with a clean, well loaded brush. Let the stain penetrate, usually five to 15 minutes. When the wet stain starts to glaze on the surface or become dull, it's

time to wipe it off. Use a coarse, absorbent cloth and wipe wood as clean as you can. It may take a little muscle power. The longer you leave on the stain, the darker the final finish will be. Again, make a few tests where it won't hurt anything before applying it to the refinishing project if you are at all particular about the final color.

If the color is not dark enough after 20 or 30 minutes of soaking in, it probably means you used the wrong color stain in the first place. Either add black pigment or go to a stain that shows up darker on the color chart, no matter what the label says it is. Wiping stains can be blended to get almost any color.

If you apply a wiping stain to a piece of furniture and then decide it is too dark, you can lighten it quite a bit by washing it down with turpentine or paint thinner and wiping it all off. This also works on a small scale for lightening small areas that may be too dark because of peculiarities in grain.

After the piece has been wiped as clean as possible, give the stain 24 hours to dry before applying the final finish. Before you go to the final topcoat, check your brand of wiping stain carefully. Many wiping stains include resin sealers which may make the next step of sealing the wood pores unnecessary. However, if you want a fine, built-up, final finish, you will probably be better off applying another sealer coat before the final topcoat. Sealers are covered in the next section.

Pigmented wiping stains are best for porous woods like fir and pine. On close grained woods they are not very effective. If it is a close grained soft wood, it absorbs too much stain over all. If it is a close grain hardwood, it won't absorb enough.

Applying a NGR Stain—Many refinishers consider NGR and water stains to be too tricky for the amateur. They are not. It is true that a pigmented wiping stain work more slowly and gives you some recourse if you botch the job, but when you think about it, there is no stain that can't be somehow fixed up. Probably the real reason that nobody is promoting the virtues of NGR and water stains is that there's no profit in it. Whereas, a lot of paint manufacturers are getting rich selling pigmented wiping stains.

The first step with an NGR stain (as with any other) is the test. Dilute the NGR stain in its solvent and apply evenly with a clean brush that is fully loaded with stain. Don't skimp. Let the stain dry for at least four hours before trying to judge it. If it's too light, try a stronger solution. Or, if you aren't testing, apply a second coat over the first. One of the nice things about NGR stains is that they don't seal the wood, so the effect is cumulative. If the wood appears too dark, flood the surface with solvent and wipe clean. If that doesn't lighten it enough, you will have to bleach it, as explained in the next section. If you have been testing, however, all you need do to lighten it is dilute the NGR stain more before applying it to the furniture.

Allow NGR stains to dry at least four hours before going to the next step in finishing, which is usually applying a sealer coat.

NGR stain is best for close grained woods like maple and birch although they produce brilliantly clear color in almost all woods.

Applying a Water Stain—These are handled in a similar manner to NGR stains in application. The difference is that water tends to raise the grain of the wood. If the wood was properly sanded, wetted down and then resanded to remove the raised grain before the water stain was applied, there will be very little grain left to raise up. When it does raise, it can be knocked off with a very light sanding with 6/0 or 7/0 sandpaper. Be sure to sand lightly, or you will remove some of the stain and change its color somewhat. Wait until the wood is completely dry before sanding, usually 24 hours.

Water stain, like the NGR, should be applied with a large clean brush and kept fully loaded. Try to keep the surface being stained flat and level if possible so the stain won't run. However, do not let it stand in puddles since this causes a difference in shade. When you have to work on a vertical surface, work with plenty of stain in the brush and work quickly so drips won't have time to sink in.

Water stain is best for woods that only need light coloring such as mahogany, cherry and walnut, although it is suitable for most woods and produces brilliant colors similar to, but slightly cooler than an NGR stain.

HOW TO MAKE WOOD LIGHTER

If the wood you are finishing is too dark for any reason, it is quite simple to make it lighter. There are two basic ways to go about it: 1. use a bleach or 2. use a lightener stain.

Lightener stain—This is really a pigmented wiping stain that happens to have very light or white pigments instead of dark ones. Like all wiping stains, the pigments are absorbed into the soft parts of the wood, making the entire surface look lighter. They are applied, allowed to glaze over and then wiped off, leaving the soft parts full of pigment. These work best on coarse grained woods. Lightening stain is sold under brand names like *White Rez, White Firzite* and ash-colored *Tonetic Wood Stain* by Pratt and Lambert.

There are other ways to add light pigments to wood. Old fashioned pickling of oak was just white paint brushed on, allowed to set up slightly, then wiped off. A white or light wood filler can be used to fill the wood pores and lighten the look of the wood. Fillers are covered in a later section.

BLEACHING WOOD

Lightening stains add pigments that are light. Bleaching removes pigments that are dark, just the way laundry bleach

One soaking with laundry bleach produced this much difference in color in a piece of pine that was fairly white to begin with. More bleach will cause more whitening.

Laundry bleach is used to remove stains on wood. Ammonia, hydrogen peroxide, benzine and other things can be tried if stain does not respond. Restain lightened wood.

does. In fact, laundry bleach works reasonably well on wood.

Laundry bleach—Ordinary *Clorox* will remove a lot of the natural pigmentation from wood. Use it full strength, giving it 20 or 30 minutes to work. If the first dose doesn't make the wood light enough, repeat. The effect is cumulative. Don't sand between bleachings or you'll remove some of what you've bleached. Laundry bleach is slow compared to other things but it does give you more control because you work in successive applications.

Ammonia will also bleach wood to some extent and can be used in the same way as *Clorox*.

Both ammonia and chlorine bleaches should be rinsed thoroughly from wood's surface when the wood is bleached enough to suit you.

Oxalic Acid—This mild acid is stronger than laundry bleaches and should be applied while wearing rubber gloves. You can get oxalic acid powder at most good paint stores. To make it full strength, dissolve as much of the crystals as possible in water. Apply freely with a large brush, let stand 15 or 20 minutes, then rinse with clear water. It not only lightens wood but also is great for spot-removing rust, alkali and other stains. After rinsing, neutralize surface with a wash of white vinegar, a cup of borax in a quart of water or ammonia diluted 10 to one.

Two-Part Bleach—This is a special, powerful type that gets most wood light enough in a single operation. You get

them at good paint stores or mail-order houses catering to woodworkers. They come in two bottles, imaginatively labelled No. 1 and No. 2. You apply No. 1 first and then No. 2. At least it's logical.

It is especially important that the wood be clean and free of grease, wax or dirt, since this will impede the bleaching action and show up as a bad discoloration. Flow on No. 1 solution with large nylon brush. Make sure it soaks in evenly all over. If any spots resist penetration, rough them up very slightly with extra fine steel wool. Let No. 1 solution soak in for about 20 minutes then apply No. 2 solution. If you use the same brush, wash it out thoroughly between applications. Let No. 2 dry thoroughly. When it's dry, the bleaching action is complete. Wash with clear water and again let dry completely. It will probably require sanding again since the bleaching action is so powerful. Use 6/0 sandpaper and go lightly so as not to remove the bleached surface wood, only raised grain.

It is important here, too, to read the specific manufacturer's instructions. Some types require you to mix No. 1 and No. 2 solutions just before applying them to the wood, for example. Also wear rubber gloves to protect your skin.

SEALER COAT

After you stained or bleached the wood and smoothed down any grain that has been raised, you are ready for the sealer coat, also known as the primer coat. There are several reasons why a sealer coat is desireable: it gives the final finish coat a good, sound surface to adhere to; it saves on the final finishing material by filling pores with less expensive stuff, and it locks in the stain to prevent it from creeping up into the final finish and making it muddy.

A popular type of wood sealer is just shellac which has been thinned slightly.It is inexpensive, readily obtainable and fast drying. It does not have as good adhesive qualities as lacquer or synthetic sealers.

Clear lacquer which has been thinned slightly also makes an excellent wood sealer. It dries fast and does not darken the wood appreciably. It makes an excellent base for the top coat to adhere to. Some dealers such as Pryme also contain lighteners which assure you of a finish that is not darkened at all.

Because of its superior adhesion, clear varnish, which has been thinned considerably, makes an acceptable sealer for wood that is to have a filler. Fillers tend to reduce adhesion. The disadvantages of a varnish sealer are that it tends to darken wood, it takes a long time to dry and some topcoats, such as lacquer, will not go over it without crinkling when dry.

Whatever sealer you use, the final step after it dries completely is a very light sanding with 7/0 garnet paper and a good dusting.

WOOD FILLERS

Wood fillers are controversial. Some finishing experts think wood looks lousy unless the pores in the wood are filled with some material to make the surface mirror flat. Other experts think that fillers destroy the natural look of the wood and give it an artificial, muddy appearance. Everyone agrees that a filler tends to reduce the adhesive qualities of the top coat over it. Traditional finishing materials tend to chip and flake when there is a filler between them and the wood. And modern finishes such as Fabulor just will not stick to paste fillers.

There are two basic types of wood filler —liquid and paste. Liquid fillers are actually nothing more than wood sealers with some silicate solids stirred in. They are just fine for fine grained woods, but then fine grained woods hardly need filled anyway. You apply it with a brush like any top coating, only work a little thinner perhaps. When it is completely dry, sand off the top with 5/0 and then 7/0 sandpaper. Don't sand to the wood or you'll just open up new pores, not to mention remove the stain. Actually, the sanding sealer you put on after the stain or bleach probably filled the pores of close grained wood anyway.

Paste wood fillers are another story. They can be obtained in all the standard wood colors, like stains, plus black, white and primary colors. They can be mixed to make in-between colors. Or you can buy neutral paste filler and pigments separately. Then when you need some, mix up a batch of the exact color you need. You won't be stuck with odd colored leftovers.

Paste fillers are generally used on coarse grained woods such as oak and mahogany. The accompanying chart will help you decide when to use it.

In selecting a paste wood filler, most people want a color that is the same as, but slightly darker than the stain they are using. Thus if you use a standard maple stain, the compatible maple-colored filler will be slightly darker.

As it comes from the pan, paste fillers are thick and pasty. They must be thinned for use to the consistency of heavy cream. Apply with a brush, using back and forth and sideways strokes to make sure every pore is filled. Let the filler set for about 30 minutes and when it starts to dull over on top, squeegee off all you can with a piece of cardboard or rubber squeegee.

When the filler has dried for 24 hours, touch up the surface lightly with 6/0 sandpaper and dust it with vacuum and tack rag or other clean cloth. The wood is now ready for the finish coat.

PASTE FILLER WOOD CHART

Do not use paste filler		OK to use paste filler	
Basswood	Cedar		
Cypress	Beech		
Birch	Fir	Ash	Chestnut
Hemlock	Gum	Oak	Elm
Pine	Poplar	Hickory	Locust
Willow	Maple	Butternut	Mahogany
Spruce	Sycamore	Walnut	Rosewood

Good wood deserves tender treatment. The warm wood tones were restored nicely here.

THE CLEAR FINISHES

With shellac, lacquer, varnish or new resin finishes, you can make nearly any surface

The problem of determining which of the clear finishes to use must be solved in terms of the "look" you want to achieve and the use to which the furniture piece will be put. The unfinished look of a penetrating resin would not be right for a Chippendale table, for example. A beautiful rubbed shellac finish would be completely destroyed by alcohol if used on a bar or cocktail table. The three principal choices are shellac, lacquer and varnish. Two others are also used quite often, rubbed oil finishes and penetrating resin finishes. And of course there are combinations of finishes. Study them all and decide which is most appropriate to your project.

115

Shellac is a natural product with a somewhat limited shelf-life so most of the top brands stamp a use-date on the top of can. Old shellac may not harden quickly or at all.

SHELLAC DILUTION CHART

Cut purchased	Alcohol to be added per quart
To end with one-pound cut	
5-Pound cut	⅔ gal.
4-pound cut	2 qts.
3-Pound cut	3 pts.
2-Pound cut (not commercially available)	1 qt.
To end with two-pound cut	
5-Pound cut	1 qt.
4-Pound cut	¾ qt.
3-Pound cut	¾ pt.
To end with three-pound cut	
5-Pound cut	⅞ pt.
4-Pound cut	½ pt.

SHELLAC

The advantages of shellac are so numerous it has remained one of the favorites of furniture finishers for a couple hundred years. It is economical, it dries fast, it flexes without cracking or chipping, it has impact resistance, it adheres well to wood, itself and other finishing materials, it builds up to a deep finish, it can be rubbed to a very high polish and the color of white shellac is clear with a beautiful touch of warmth and character. Orange shellac produces a look similar to varnish.

The disadvantages of a shellac finish are basically one thing: it has little resistance to water and alcohol. It must be waxed heavily but even that may not suffice for surfaces like dining tabletops. Also, new urethane resin varnish won't go on well over it but you can look at this as a disadvantage of urethane varnish if you like.

BUYING SHELLAC

The two things to remember about buying shellac is (1) don't buy more than you need for a specific job and (2) don't use it as it comes from the jar or can.

The reason for #1 is that shellac doesn't keep. After a time chemical changes take place which prevent it from setting properly and ruin its durability.

Don't take chances buying unknown brands which the store may have had on its shelves for months. A fast-selling known brand is usually safe. Many, such as Zinsser Bulls Eye Shellac, have the use date stamped on the can top. If you should have some shellac on hand of unknown vintage, test it on scrap wood before using. It should set hard in 30 minutes. If not, throw the stuff out. It's cheap enough.

The reason for #2, above, is that shellac almost always needs to be thinned with denatured alcohol. Some brands say "ready to use" on the label which probably means it is "three pound cut", a consistancy which can easily be used by experienced finishers. Beginners and many experts prefer to use shellac that is one- or two-pound cut, which means thinning.

The "cut" of shellac merely indicated the number of pounds of resin dissolved in a gallon of alcohol. Thus, the usual three-pound cut shellac means it has three pounds of resin per gallon. In practice, you're likely to find shellac put up in three-, four- or five-pound cuts. The following chart will help you in making dilutions.

HOW TO APPLY SHELLAC

Start with one-pound cut shellac because it goes on easier, dries faster, is more tolerant of mistakes and builds up to a finer finish than fewer coats of heav-

For touch up and small areas, shellac in aerosol spray cans is convenient and does a fine job. Move can back and forth to prevent drips, sags. If possible, lay work flat.

Wax is absolutely necessary to protect shellac finishes where there is any contact with moisture, including damp air. Shellac absorbs water, turns cloudy; wax protects.

ier shallac. Stir, don't shake, to prevent bubbles.

With the wood sanded, stained and filled, wipe clean with soft, lintless cloth or tack rag. Use clean brush that is wide enough to do the job without too many fussy little strokes. Keep the brush fully loaded and flow the shallac on in long straight strokes, lapping each one.

Allow one to two hours for the first coat to dry before sanding. In very humid weather, it may take longer. Then sand off with sanding block and 6/0 garnet paper, using an open-coat type so it won't clog as quickly. If you use a better type garnet or silicon carbide paper, it can be washed clean with alcohol and used again. Flint paper will disintegrate.

After sanding the first coat, wipe away all dust carefully, and apply a second coat of shellac. Since there is no longer bare wood under it to absorb the alcohol, this coat will take longer, probably two to three hours. When it is dry, sand again, this time more lightly. Subsequent coats are treated like the second coat. There should be at least three coats using one-pound cut and tops of tables and dressers should have five. The number is partly a matter of personal preference. Shellac coats weld together and can be built up into beautifully thick, translucent surfaces. With more experience and less patience, you will be able to apply shellac as thick as three-pound cut.

After the last coat is on, rub it down with 4/0 steel wool, working along the grain lightly. This will produce a matte finish. It should then be left to dry for at least 24 hours and waxed. Always use a good paste wax and buff with soft cloth or buffing sleeve on an electric drill sanding wheel. After buffing, apply a second coat of wax and buff again. Wax is very important because shellac turns white when water hits it. With the wax, a shellac finish can be made very glossy if desired.

CLEANING UP

Immediately after use, wash brushes with denatured alcohol or household ammonia and water. In either case, then wash with soap and warm water. Align and shape bristles and allow to dry undisturbed.

FRENCH POLISHING

There are many systems for French polishing and they generally fall into two categories: those which produce a nice finish and those which keep the finisher busy for hours. We will skip the pure, time-honored methods in favor of a faster method which produces about the same results. In fact, better results if you aren't skilled at it.

First, prepare the wood and wipe absolutely free of dust. Rub or paint on three layers of one-pound cut shellac, allowing drying time and sanding between coats. Then, with a pad made of a ball of soft clean rags, apply the. French coat. This is done by dipping the pad in one-pound cut shellac and adding a few drops of boiled linseed oil to the center of the pad.

Start rubbing with a circular motion without stopping. As it is absorbed, run the pad off the surface without stopping and add more shellac and boiled linseed oil. Then start making circular motions with the pad and ease it onto the surface again. When the entire surface is covered this way, allow 24 hours to dry and repeat. Keep repeating until the finish is pleasing to you. The more you work, the more you'll find yourself pleased with just what you've got. To remove the oil after the final coat, use a turpentine-soaked rag, rung as dry as possible. Or an alcohol-soaked rag, although don't do more than whisk across in this case, since alcohol can wipe it all off. Or just use a soft cloth.

LACQUER

Historically, lacquer was invented as an improvement on shellac. Its advantages, however, apply mostly to furniture production in factories using spray equipment. These mostly involve fast drying.

Spraying lacquer is used by home craftsmen, of course, but the advantages of this type lacquer certainly does not warrant buying paint spraying equipment.

Brushing lacquers are now readily available to home craftsmen and produce probably the highest gloss finish that can be built up with brush and polishing abrasives. A common brushing lacquer is *Fabulon,* which is also used for floors. There are other brands, usually with the letters "l-a-c" somewhere in the brand name.

The advantages of brushing lacquer are: dries quickly so it doesn't collect much dust; leaves wood almost undarkened; achieves highest sheen and is more resistant to water and alcohol than shellac. On the other side, however, it can chip and peel if not properly applied, it dries so fast it may be difficult for some workers to apply. Lacquer also contains solvents which cause some stains and wood fillers to bleed into the top coats, making them muddy. In fact, lacquer solvents will dissolve the pigments out of rosewood, mahogany and some other woods. To prevent this bleeding, give at least 48 hours drying time for fillers, use only NGR or water stains and seal wood with shellac first.

APPLYING LACQUER

The wood should be properly prepared, as covered in earlier chapters. Wipe free of dust with tack rag or clean cloth.

When buying lacquer, buy at least as much lacquer thinner. Never work with lacquer that doesn't flow on easily, which means that most of the time you will have to thin it.

Use a clean brush that is wide enough to cover the job in as few as possible strokes. A lacquer brush is wider and thinner than a varnish brush, without having to have the long bristles. Load the brush well and flow the lacquer on quickly. Work narrow areas, keeping the edges wet and lapped. On large jobs, the beginning will be dry to the touch before you finish it.

Although lacquer will set in minutes, allow four hours at least before you sand or apply a second coat. Sanding should be very light, only to knock down any bubbles, specks of dust or grain that has risen. It is not needed for adhesion, as is the case with varnish. Sanding should be with flat sanding block to level up the finish only. Do not use water in wet sanding. The last coat may be rubbed with pumice and oil as outlined later in this chapter. The result of careful application in thin coats, sanding with 6/0 and finer papers on a good flat sanding block and finish rubbing with oil and pumice is the highest polish of any finish a home craftsman can achieve.

VARNISH

Varnish is about the toughest, most durable, water-resistant, heat-resistant finish you can put on. Some of the modern polyurethane varnishes are almost clear, although others show somewhat warmer. The trouble with varnish is that it's a pain to put on. Chemical science has achieved

Perhaps the glossiest finish possible for the home refinisher is produced by French polishing. There are several methods but easiest uses shellac, linseed oil and a polishing ball.

After French polishing ball is dipped in 1-pound oil shellac, a few drops of raw linseed oil are added. It is rubbed onto surface with continuous circular motion to complete.

great strides toward making it easier, however. Most of the troubles in application stem from the fact that a coat of varnish takes at least 24 hours to dry enough to sand and often 48 hours. There are now fast drying types that set in two hours. Some types of varnish are affected drastically by sunlight while others deteriorate in time due to oxidation. They crack, craze and become brittle.

TYPES OF VARNISHES

Synthetics have almost completely replaced the old natural resin varnishes and with them went many of the traditional problems. Perhaps the best all around synthetic resin varnish is polyurethane which has the best combination of durability, long life, water-like clarity, finished polish, good flexibility and shortened drying time. It will not, however, go on well over shellac.

Epoxy varnishes are extremely durable and are perhaps the easiest to brush on. Some brands of epoxy varnish like *Sapolin Triple Duty Varnish* claims to dry in two hours. Other synthetics upon which varnishes are based are alkyds, phenolics and vinyls. The latter features great clearness and excellent flexibility.

Another type which someone mistakenly used on furniture from time to time is spar varnish. Don't use it. Except on spars, where it remains flexible and re-

sistant to weather. It can't be properly finished and some types never dry completely.

Most varnishes are labelled "Glossy", "Satin" or "Flat". The "glossy" is untreated varnish. "Satin" and "Flat" are treated to have either a matte or flat look when dry. Sometimes this is achieved by silica flakes stirred in. You can tell by the inch or so of sand-like stuff in the bottom of the can which must be stirred into suspension. This type varnish is rather old-fashioned and not as durable as glossy varnish. Since it is not completely clean, several coats of it can obscure the grain. If you are using it, do so only on the last coat.

Modern "satin" and "flat" varnishes achieve their look through chemicals included in the varnish formula and can be used just like glossy varnish without worry.

HOW TO APPLY VARNISH

After the wood is sanded, stained and otherwise prepared, test in some inconspicuous place to see how the varnish will look. If it is too dark, which often happens, buy a clearer type varnish if you don't already have it. Otherwise, remove some of the stain to lighten it, as described earlier.

If you are applying varnish over previously finished furniture, wash the old finish with detergent, rinse thoroughly and

119

wipe dry. Then lightly sand entire surface to effect bonding and wipe away all dust before applying varnish. Or you can use a bonding agent such as Klean-Strip's *No Sand* which softens, cleans and degreases the old finish so the varnish will bond well.

THE DUST PROBLEM

Dust is public enemy number 1 to varnishers. You think a room is dust-free until you start to varnish. And suddenly there are specks and flecks all over your new finish.

Cure No. 1 is to work in the most dust free room you can find. An empty guest room is pretty good. Put the furniture piece in the room and clean it thoroughly with vacuum cleaner, tack rag or anything else that will catch dust. Then leave the room for three or four hours. Let the dust settle.

When you get ready to varnish, remember that clothes carry dust. And if you start stomping around in wool clothing, you'll be making your own dust as you work. It is said that old-time coach makers stripped naked before applying varnish. Clean clothing made of synthetic material are pretty good, but don't move around too much. And wipe frequently with tack rag as you work.

BRUSHING ON VARNISH

Most varnishes can be used as it comes from the can. If it is used as a sealer too, that coat should be diluted 20 per cent with turps or paint thinner. If you used a sealing stain, don't dilute the varnish. When the varnish seems to drag on the brush, it should be thinned slightly to correct this. Don't shake. Stir carefully to avoid bubbles.

A varnish brush should be fuller and have longer bristles than those used for shellac and lacquer. Dip the brush half way up the bristles and strike off the dripping. Lay down the varnish in long, thin strips in alternate stripes, like a zebra. Then go back and cross them and finally fill in between by brushing out lap marks. Since varnish sets up slowly compared to

shellac and lacquer, you have time to work. At the ends of tops and sides, tip off the excess to keep a bead or "fat lip" from building up. Use the tip of the brush, slightly dry.

Most finishers do their varnishing while working against a window or light background so they can see what's happening by the reflected light on the glossy new surface.

Places that are likely to hold little reservoirs of varnish, such as corners and carvings, should be brushed once with a wet brush to put the varnish on, and once with a brush that has been thoroughly worked dry, to remove excess varnish in crevices.

Despite your best efforts, into each life some lint must fall. Therefore you'll need a lint picker. Old timers make this by putting a little ball of soft rosin on the end of a match stick. Musical or baseball rosin will do. Melt it in hot water and ball it up on the end of the stick. Then touch the rosin to each speck of lint that falls and it will come away clean. You can also pick lint with an artists brush, slightly wet. When brush bristles fall, pick them up with two sticks.

After the varnish completely covers the piece, leave the room and seal it for 24 hours. Or, in damp weather, 36 to 48 hours. However, it is important to read the instructions on the varnish can. Some of the new types dry enough to be lint free in a couple of hours. And others require that a second coat be applied *before* the first one dries for the sake of adhesion.

But assuming a standard varnish, let it dry thoroughly and completely. The longer the better. Then sand between coats, using 6/0 open coat garnet paper. As always, use a flat sanding block to level the surface and knock off any raised grain, bubbles or flecks of dust that may have landed. Any low spots that are not roughed up by the sanding block should be hit lightly with fine steel wool so the next coat will adhere properly. Let each coat dry 24 to 48 hours before sanding again. Build up three to six coats this way and end up with wet abrasives like pumice and oil followed by rottenstone and oil, applied with felt pad, and you've got the classic piano finish.

Expert refinishers try to keep window or bright light lined up with surface so they will quickly see and void any specks or bubbles.

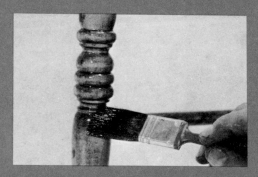

Turnings hold some of the finish in the cracks which drip and mar the end result. Use tip of brush to remove excess finish.

PENETRATING RESIN FINISHES

These are not considered finishes at all by some. They were formulated to sink into the wood, sealing the pores and hardening the fibers near the surface. They serve as excellent sealers, obviously, but they provide excellent final finish as well, as long as you know that's what you want. It won't give a built up finish that looks as if a sheet of glass were glued to the surface. But if you like wood that looks truly natural and still resists normal wear and tear, penetrating resin finishes are excellent. And when marred, just add a little more and it blends in perfectly.

To apply a penetrating resin finish, you just pour it on. Then work it in with a little pad of steel wool or soft cloth. Keep the surface wet with the resin for 30 minutes or more while it soaks in. Then wipe it away. After 24 hours, do it again, and perhaps a third time for areas that get a lot of action. And that's all. Since the penetrating resin is crystal clear, the effect on wood is about the same as water. A slight darkening. Of course NGR or water stain can be applied first, as with any other finish.

Penetrating resin finishes are sold under brand names like *Clear Reg, Clear Miniwax* and *Deep Finish Firzite*.

ANTIQUE OIL FINISH

Boiled linseed oil does make a furniture finish. And people fight over whether it's wonderful or terrible. That's a matter of opinion but it is not a matter of debate that it is old and it is interesting.

Mix one part boiled linseed oil and one part distilled turpentine. Heat them (in double boiler and beware of fire) together and apply to the wood surface, keeping it wet for two days until it can drink no more. Then sprinkle down the surface with powdered pumice and rub down with burlap or other rough cloth. Do this a couple of times and then apply pure linseed oil and rottenstone powder. When all the rottenstone is wiped away, let the oil set a week and apply paste wax. Then buff to a high gloss.

A simpler version of the oil finish is to apply the hot linseed oil-turpentine to the wood, let it soak in and wipe dry and polish with soft cloth. Give it several applications the first day, wiping and polishing in between. Then five daily applications and 12 monthly applications. The resulting finish is not particularly durable and it certainly is not all that easy to put on. So you have to like its looks to do it.

121

Antiquing or glazing is one of the most popular forms of painted furniture. This composite photo shows the three simple steps: the base coat; wipe-off glaze coat and clear sealer coat.

FINISHES IN COLOR

If wood doesn't deserve a clear finish, or if a room demands color, consider "paint"

Many people don't realize that their provincial antiques were originally painted by the maker or first owner. A clear finish just wasn't practical until the advent of good shellacs, lacquers and varnishes. But good paint has been the mainstay of furniture finishing for a thousand years or more. So don't sneer at opaque color finishes. And don't feel bad if your furniture project is so ungraceful that there's nothing to do but "paint" it. Beautiful, durable, lustrous finishes can be built up with enamel, lacquer and the new plastic coatings.

ENAMEL

Enamel is just varnish with pigment in it. You put it on the same way, as described in detail in the previous section.

In buying enamel, it doesn't pay to go for the cheapest thing on the market. In general with enamels, you get what you pay for. And in working relatively small areas such as are involved in furniture finishing, it doesn't pay. Get a brand name you can trust. Enamels are available in Glossy, Semi-Gloss and Flat. Don't even consider flat enamel for furniture. Semi-Gloss is acceptable, although not always recommended. The reason is that Glossy enamel is the most durable. That's because the chemicals which remove the glossy sheen also have a *slightly* detrimental effect on durability. And when a piece of furniture must flex, as with rattan furniture or flexible back slats, Glossy enamel is a must. Also, the darker enamel colors only come in Glossy. Glossy enamel can be made semi-gloss or even flat by rubbing the final coat with 7/0 garnet paper or 4/0 steel wool.

Like varnish, enamel should be applied in coats. At least three. Some refinishers use an undercoat on bare wood because it is cheaper but this is not necessary. Enamel adheres very well to any clean wood surface. And a white undercoat (which most undercoatings are) will show through many top coats of enamel, so it must be tinted to the shade of darker enamels, at least. Fillers are not needed for most woods because enamel pigments do the filling.

Apply the first coat of enamel, slightly thinned, to the bare wood, properly finished. And don't skimp on the wood finishing just because a color is going on over it. A bad job will show up even more in color because there's no grain showing to fool the eye. After the first coat has dried thoroughly, 24 hours for most types of enamel, sand it down with 4/0 open coat garnet paper. Then apply the second coat of enamel without thinning. When it has dried thoroughly for 24 hours (depending on type), sand again lightly with 6/0 garnet paper. And apply the third coat.

Dust is as much a problem with enamel finishes as it is with varnish. Work in a room that is as dust free as you can find. And keep people out while the enamel is drying. While you paint wear dust-free clothing and don't move around any more than necessary. And dust that lands as you are painting should be picked out of the enamel immediately.

The final finish can be rubbed like varnish or left glossy. If you want the final surface to be semi-glossy, you can use Semi-Gloss for the last coat, although you will get a better finish if you use Glossy and flatten it with sandpaper. If you want to smooth the top coat, it can then be made glossier with rottenstone and oil, followed by waxing, as described earlier.

SHELLAC AND LACQUER IN COLOR

In general, you won't find *brushing lacquers* in colors. That's because they are applied so thin that they won't hold much pigment. Therefore many coats must be

Epoxy enamel makes a very smooth and tough coating for furniture. With proper sanding between coats, it takes on high gloss; is resistant to heat, abrasion and chemicals.

Japan colors are used to tint lacquer. The end result is very shiny but it must be built up in many layers because lacquer has to be very thin for brushing. Keep down dust.

One of handiest ways to apply lacquer is with aerosol can. This type is used by graphic artists but is suitable for small furniture. Auto spray lacquers are also excellent.

Kits are available for antiquing furniture. There are many combinations of base coat colors and glazes. These ingredients can be purchased separately at most paint stores.

In antiquing, the glaze coat is brushed on roughly after the base coast has thoroughly dried. After glaze coat starts to dull on top, wipe away high spots for antique effect.

put on to achieve the opacity needed for most jobs. The law of diminishing returns then applies and it's quicker and easier to just put on two or three coats of enamel.

You can do it however. Just purchase the proper pigments, such as Japan colors (available from the mail order supply houses like Constantine's), and mix them according to specific instructions on the tube or package into the clear lacquer. And go to work putting on multi coats.

SPRAY LACQUERS

Spraying colored lacquer is very practical, however, and is done by furniture manufacturers all the time. For the home craftsman, the spray can lacquers, such as *Krylon* or *DuPont Spray Paint*, are more practical unless you have a lot to do.

The best quality aerosol spray lacquers are available from auto supply stores. The cans that match the car colors. There are hundreds of colors and they are of the best durability.

In using spray can lacquers, always put them on in many thin coats to prevent sagging and uneven build-up. In general, hold the can upright with nozzel 12″ to 15″ from the work. Do not try to spray on enamel when room temperature is over 85° or below 65°, although this varies with type. Also, some spray lacquers will not hold second coats well unless applied

within 30 minutes. Read directions carefully, of course.

EPOXY COATINGS

There are now very durable epoxy enamels which must be mixed with a hardener. A catalytic action occurs which makes the coating extremely durable. Colors are generally bright and hold well and the drying time is fast enough that dust is not as much of a problem as with enamels. However, sanding between coats is difficult and the finish is not as beautiful. Epoxy enamels are suitable for outdoor furniture, kitchen furniture and children's furniture.

ANTIQUING

This is the process that artists call glazing. It is a base coat, in a color, followed by another coat which is rubbed away enough to let the base coat show through. Most paint stores supply all the materials in kit form. The reason people call it "antiquing" is that the top coat is usually umber or sienna or something dark that suggests age, rather than paint. Antiquing is perfect for old furniture that is not either valuable or beautiful but you have to do *something*. It's done a lot with unpainted furniture.

The first step, as always, is to prepare the wood well. Here, however is a variation. After sanding completely, as de-

Glaze coat is not durable or glossy and must be protected by a clear sealer coat. It comes with every kit or can be purchased separately. Do not neglect this important step.

Antiquing has made this cheap unpainted hutch base into a featured entry-way piece. The glaze coat topped by the sealer coat makes it very durable for this hard service.

scribed previously, the surface can be distressed to emphasize the "antique" myth. Whip it with chains, shoot it with bird shot, stab it with an ice pick, wear down the wear spots with a rasp, and so on. Sand the wounds, dust and you're ready for the base coat. These blemishes will hold the glaze coat and show up as worm holes, wear spots and unknown wear and tear. Supposedly.

Some antiquers apply a primer coat although this is not necessary as the enamel base coat adheres very well. If the piece is already painted or has a sound finish, use a paint bonding deglosser such as *No Sand* (made by Klean-Strip) so your base coat will adhere to the previous finish. Otherwise you will have to rough up the entire old surface with 4/0 sandpaper. *No Sand* also cleans the wood and, incidentally, is a great household cleaner as well.

The base coat should be made as fine as any enamel finish, in the opinion of many experts. Some think that a sloppy base coat will show up as "antique" but it doesn't. Just sloopy.

After the base coat is thoroughly dry, a glaze coat is put on. Here you can achieve some beautiful effects if you forget the myth of "antique" looks. Gold glazed with red, for example. Blue glazed with white. Yellow glazed with orange. And so on. The usual antique glaze is an earth color, burnt umber or sienna, often with

black mixed in. You can use color pigments thinned a little in turpentine, if you give it plenty of time to dry. Of stir the pigments into clear resin sealer and use that as your glaze. Or you can buy readymade glazes at most paint stores nowadays. And of course, you can buy the whole works in kit form.

The glaze coat can be applied sloppily just as long as you cover every square inch of surface. Work the glaze into all the corners, cracks, worm holes and other indentations. Let the glaze set up until the surface starts to turn dull and start rubbing it away with a soft cloth. If it isn't dry enough, wait. Start wiping in the center of the flat surfaces and work to the edges in a circular motion. Wipe all the high spots and leave all the indentations. Where it would show wear or highlights, wipe off the glaze. Leave it in the corners and edges and grade it away in-between. If you goof, wash it all off with turpentine and start over.

Once the wiping is done to your liking, it can be "grained " by dragging a dry, poor-condition brush lightly across it. This takes practice, however. Experiment a little first. When the glaze coat is completely dry, say in 48 to 72 hours, it must be sealed. Use a semi-gloss polyurethane varnish if you want the usual effect. There is nothing wrong with glossy urethane varnish as a sealer if you like it shiny.

INDEX

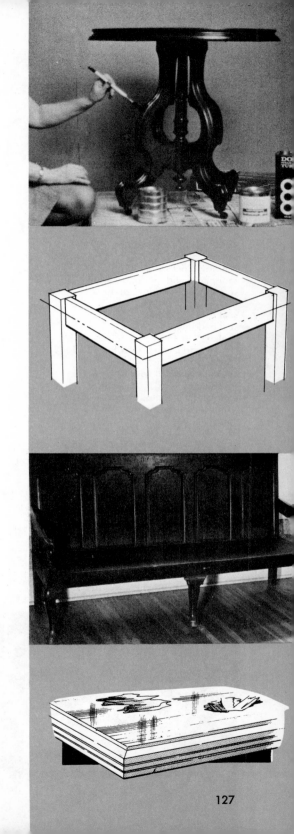